FOR GRANTED

TO THE GIRL WHO HAVE A SPECIAL PLACE IN MY HEART

NAYAN HEDAU

Copyright © Nayan Hedau
All Rights Reserved.

This book has been published with all efforts taken to make the material error-free after the consent of the author. However, the author and the publisher do not assume and hereby disclaim any liability to any party for any loss, damage, or disruption caused by errors or omissions, whether such errors or omissions result from negligence, accident, or any other cause.

While every effort has been made to avoid any mistake or omission, this publication is being sold on the condition and understanding that neither the author nor the publishers or printers would be liable in any manner to any person by reason of any mistake or omission in this publication or for any action taken or omitted to be taken or advice rendered or accepted on the basis of this work. For any defect in printing or binding the publishers will be liable only to replace the defective copy by another copy of this work then available.

To the person whose *unconditional love* & support changed the course of
my life.

To my Unforgettable love, *Pakhi.*

Wonders if I am writing about *her.*

Yes I am.

Contents

Foreword

This is the story of a heart I broke. I always felt I was the one who broke into pieces. but you know what in fact I was the one who broke her into pieces. *Love isn't just an emotion.* You know we take love *for granted* maybe it is true but not the person who loved you should be taken *granted.* It's not always me. It's always him/her. They say you learn from mistakes, but I came way to far to get her back. I thought I was the one bearing. Every emotion but in fact it was her holding on to my Love. *I am sinner* who can't be forgiven. In need of punishment but *she left me unharmed* cuz she loved me. I am someone who can neither be forgiven nor be punished. I am standing on a sticky thread above the hell, neither I can balance myself nor I can fall into the hell. *Maybe this is something I deserve....*

Preface

When all is said and done, most of us are doing the best we can, and most of us don't go into relationships with the intention of messing things up. We try our best to love and be loved in return. Yet despite our best intentions, when we do mess things up, it most likely is because we disregarded, dismissed, or didn't know about at least one of the parts described in this book. This should give hope to the reader because, the truth is, you can still be wired for love, if not in this relationship, then in the next one. It is never too late.

And there is no one reading this book who can't ultimately do it right.

Couples have more options, and more resources at their fingertips.

The universe keeps pitching us new opportunities to redo, repair, and reinvent ourselves in relationship to another person, perhaps even the same person.

We just need to envision a more principled reason to be together, a more life- enhancing purpose to devote ourselves to another person. This purpose must be based on true mutuality; on giving ourselves fully to our chosen other; and on the willingness to accept one another as we are, with all our irritating qualities.

Acknowledgements

My sincere thanks to the following people, for taking me ahead in the journey of writing this book.

Shezan, for reviewing this book for the very first time even in the midnight and helping me with the first edit work.

Pakhi's Mom, Who were always there for me, I always have their back, no matters what mistakes I have done, they never judged me and still loving me as the same.

Ifham, for always motivating me and supporting me in my toughest times and thank you for always being there for me.

Hitanshu, Om and Jay, my roommates, my good friends, for being punctual at the 3'o clock in the morning that I can do it.

Sanjana and Priti, my cutest and dearest friend, for being the kind of a reader who can be any writer's delight. For always keeping my spirits up and showing me the better ways to bring this book up.

Snoopy (Female Dog) and Eiza (Female Cat), My PETS For teaching me how to love anyone unconditionally

About Author

Pakhi, Eiza, Me & Snoopy

Myself NAYAN HEDAU currently pursuing my MBBS Degree from Yerevan Gladzor University from Armenia. My birthplace is Nagpur, Maharashtra. Presently I am in Yerevan, Armenia for MBBS Degree. I am an ex-army cadet. I am the father of two proud to say cuties *Eiza (Female Cat) and Snoopy (Female Dog)*. I am passionate about writing and have an interest in playing Badminton. I am an avid reader and have interest in music. My music taste is so good. I am having an incredible fashion sense you'd die for. I love to follow trends and I am active on social media and loves interacting with the people around me.

You can connect me on Instagram- @nynlofi & @lofinyn

One

1. Love Isn't Just An "EMOTION"

Should we leave the other person just because he/she made some mistakes?

Should we break the relationship because of it?

Should we forget the love and promises?

Should we forget the time we spent with each other?

Should we forget everything and just leave?

Should we block them from everywhere?

Should we not forgive them?

Should we?

These are the questions a broken heart wants to know the answer of.

I've heard that "Love is immortal" and if it is immortal then how does it end only after few years or months? I don't know what is wrong or what is right but when it is about love we must try again and again to save it because I know the pain it give when the person you love leaves you.

2. Do You Really Deserve Me?

Do I deserve you??

After all the things I did

All the troubles I caused

I always irritate you

I always make you angry

I hurt you a lot

Though I never plan to do any of them

All my efforts to keep you happy get backfired and I end up making you sad

And maybe the only thing I did perfectly was to dissappoint you

I annoy you a lot, I keep letting you down

I keep promising you not to do them anymore and every single time I keep
breaking them

And after all the mess I kept creating, you always found a reason to hold on

Do you really deserve an idot like me???

3. Still I Need You!

I love you....

Please listen, I don't want someone else, I just want you.

I want you during my good and bad times.

I want you to be with me, holding my hand

when everyone said "I will be there for you" leaves me, and

I can still see you and smile proudly.

I know sometimes things are hard between us but I will tolerate it all just for you.

Everytime you ask me, "If I'm tired of your weird behaviour?,

I'll still say "NO, I can't make promises to you about the moon and stars but atleast I can try to make you smile whenever I can".

Don't ask me "Why I always want you and not anybody else?", it's hard to explain,

No one can understand me better than you, no one can actually make me smile the whole day with those lovely texts.

It's not always about saying " I LOVE YOU to each other" but then whenever I see you sad it ruins my mood, those hugs which makes me feel better, I can't ever have it from someone else but I just want you.

So no matter what happens, remember "I'll always love you". I'm never ever going to leave you no matter what happens, You got it?

4. Will You Be There?

•There will be days when I'l gaze at the night sky searching for the fault in our stars and cry hereby tearing myself apart. Will you be there to take me a far?

• There will be phases when I'll lose every tincture of hope from myself, will you be there to bring a ray of hope into my hopeless soul?

• There will be sunsets worth watching alone and analysing my own downfall with tears of regret, will you be there to wipe them off and adore the beauty of endings?

• There will be cravings for coffee and maggie within me waiting for the clock to struck midnight, will you accompany me as my 2AM partner?

• There will be empty flower vases and coffee mugs kept lifelessly on the shelves, waiting to be cherished carefully and be intertwined with memories, will you help me in weaving some of the best memories together?

• There will be empty photoframes and sticky notes, waiting to be filled with colourful vibes and play ballads of our love, will you help me in painting the canvas of life?

• There will be nights when I'd be in endless riots within myself and the world will appear to be blank, will you hold me and promise to make this world a better place?

• There will be songs without beats, dance without moves and life without memories; making me curse my dark soul, will you be there to spray glitters into them and make my nights beautiful?

• There will be mornings without sunshines and nights without lights, will you walk with me in the rains and engrave our names for a "forever" ?.

5. You Own This Heart!!

You exist in me,

In my rhymes,

In my so called random thoughts.

In my veins,

In my so called beating heart.

In my routine,

In my so called busy days.

In my eyes,

In my so called far vision of Love.

In my ears,

In my so called reverberating memories.

In my words,

In my so called fascinating stories.

In my breathes,

In my so could sustaining soul.

You still exist in me.

6. She Deserves Much More Than Just "LOVE"

She is a total textbook introvert. She won't reply for hours and sometimes you won't see her for a week. You will take this personally. Don't. She's simply taking care of herself and she'll tell you how much she missed you while she was away. She'll get very jealous. My god, She gets so jealous. Those brown eyes will turn a deep green. She hates that about herself, and she doesn't mean to do it. Remember, She loves you. Reassure her that you love her too.

On that topic, she needs constant reassurance. Tell her you love her and mean it. If you can't do that, leave. She deserves more than that. There will be nights when she goes out and drinks a little too much. She'll call you to bring her home. When you do, she'll try to keep you up all night by tickling you and repeating "I love you and I'm sorry I'm annoying." She's not annoying. But make sure she has plenty of water and don't let her pass out until she drinks it, or she will be miserable in the morning. She is the most independent woman I know. But she's so insecure, it still breaks my heart. So when she starts an argument with "you don't love me." Do not get upset. Remind her you do and the reasons why. She'll come around. The cat comes first. Don't ever think otherwise. Make her tea and remember the way she takes her coffee. She will notice. When she's having an anxiety attack, wrap her up in your arms and rub her back. Tell her she's safe and remind her that she has medication if she needs it. If you cannot treat her like royalty, let someone else. That girl deserves the world. Losing her is a pain you will never shake. Your world will come crashing down on you and those pieces won't ever fit the way they used to. Don't let her go. She will love you with all she's got. Please give her the same. I am begging you to not hurt her. She is golden. Don't let that shine die out. Give her your all and she'll return the favor. You will never have to ask the universe for anything ever again.

7. *Like A Cherry Blossom Of Spring Of My Life.*

I fell in love with the way she dreamt about forever.

She was a girl of adventure and I was her writer.

She's wild, but she's soft kind of like when it rains during the winter and she smiles in such a way that makes me feel lighter.

She's a traveler filled with chaos but she feels at peace in the serenity of saltwater.

I saw a silent hope in her eyes that someday she'll recover. She's the prettiest girl in the world.

The touch of her skin feels like a mourning dove's feather.

I close my eyes, and I'm surrounded by flowers and no summer. She's my someone, my soulmate, my life.

I choose her for the reason that she inspires me to be better and today I promise that I will always cherish her in my tender

8. Like A "THORN" In My Life

I have always been too much for someone or not enough.

I'm either too loud or not loud enough. I am a walking contradiction.

A full glass or an empty one. There is no balance in me.

Tell me, what made you leave? My devastating fire or my lack of heat?

9. Old ME

I don't ask you to love me always like this,

but I ask you to remember.

Somewhere inside of me,

there will always be the person I am tonight.

10. A Beautiful Scar Hard To Erase

I think the weirdest thing is when you break up with someone and you still have this left over information about them. Like you still know their favorite song. You know their siblings' names. You remember which ice cream flavor they like and the weird dreams they told you about at 2AM. You know their dog's name and their favorite tv shows. You learned all these details about them and now they're gone. It's just weird.

11. To Be There For YOU

I love that you get cold when it's 71 degrees out.

I love that it takes you an hour and a half to order a sandwich.

I love that you get a little crinkle above your nose when you're looking at me like I'm nuts.

I love that after I spend the day with you, I can still smell your perfume on my clothes.

And I love that you are the last person I want to talk to before I go to sleep at night.

And it's not because I'm lonely. I came here tonight because when you realize you want to spend the rest of your life with somebody, then is the time you realise you want to be there for somebody.

12. Like The Fall Of A Beautiful Flower

It was August. I was looking at the twinkle in your brown eyes and your pronounced cheekbones. For that glimpse of a second I really thought we would last. You were laughing and making me laugh even more and I swear I can't verbally explain how perfect world seemed to me in that very moment. You left in April. It was a sunny day. People are so excited about the first day of summer and I'm sorry but for me every sunrise still feels like losing you.

13. You See Through Me!

You make me feel so fucking vulnerable when I am around you. I can feel how my skin breaks open, letting you see what I am truly made of. And I am made of a not so beautiful bare face, green bruises on my knuckles and a lot of enraged tears. I am made of over communication and suffocating feelings. I am made of everything and nothing. And you see right through all of it. All of it.

Thank you for loving me even when I can't love myself too.

14. Like a déjà vu

You felt familiar the moment I met you. A lovely sort of déjà vu. When we spoke or laughed or danced I became overwhelmed by the powerful sensation that I had been here before.

And when we kissed I felt the energies of a thousand lives on our lips, like our souls had known each other all along.

15. She's The One

She's the girl who has very few friends but doesn't need anymore.

She's the girl who laughs the hardest at her own jokes.

The girl who will hang up on you but then also call you right back & say 'sorry'.

She's the girl who will never leave you when you need her.

The girl who will go out of her way to cheer you up.

The girl who never sleeps without her teddy bear by her side.

She's the girl who says that she isn't ticklish, but really is.

She's that girl who won't give up on you if she really believes in you.

She's that girl who truly believes in loving someone till the last.

If you have got someone like that,

Never leave her or let her go.

16. For Me You Are The Only One

You, your eyes, your smile, your laugh, your presence…

just everything about you, I love.

In my eyes, you are totally perfect.

You're my world, my life, you mean a lot to me.

I will never let you go because I know my life won't be complete if you're
not in it.

You are my one and only.

I can't promise to fix all your problems but I promise that you will never deal with them alone.

I love you with all my heart.

Just remember that always.

17. Maybe You Truly Love My Trueself

I keep on annoying you

but you still manage

to deal with me every single time.

Sometimes I become kid who

constantly needs your attention,

Sometimes I become a mature person,

Sometimes I act dumb,

Sometimes I become sad,

Sometimes I don't believe in myself,

Sometimes I lose my confidence,

Sometimes I get very negative,

But you keep on supporting me at every stage.

Having you by my side is the best thing

that ever happened to me!

18. You Are "SPECIAL"

You know what's special?

When you hold my hand, kiss my forehead, hug me tight.

All your efforts to make me happy are special.

You're special, your love is special, our bond is special and every second I
spend with you is special and precious for me.

All the pictures we have together, every conversation, every meal we had
together, all the funny moments and every fight of ours is special in a way
that I can not forget it till my last breathe.

Yes, for me our love is special.

19. *True LOVE*

They say first love is special.

Nobody talks about 2nd love.

Is it just a compromise? No, it isn't.

It heals the wounds of 1st love.

It us more mature, more understanding

and more of everything.

Unfortunately, many fail to realise this.

20. *I LOVE YOU*

"I LOVE YOU" means that....

I accept you for the person that you are and that I don't wish to change you into someone else.

It means that I do not expect perfection from you, just as you don't expect it from me.

"I LOVE YOU" means that....

I'll stand by you through the worst times.

It means loving even when you're in bad mood.

It means loving you when you are upset, down, not just when you're fun to be with.

It means loving you till the last breath and being with you till death departs us.

21. Classic Love

No kisses,

No hugs,

No chocolates,

No expensive gifts,

No sex.

People say "Love in old times was so boring."

It wasn't boring, it was classic.

The love that was free from any kind of lust and greed.

The only thing that used to matter for those couples was love, nothing else.

Maybe, they knew the real meaning of love.

Two

1. You Make Me Special

I don't know whether its love or

something else but you are the one

with whom I can't fake my emotions,

your tight hug make me feel so safe

and just one kiss from you make me

feel wanted, your voice has that magic

which heals my pain. The way you

make efforts just to make me smile,

the way you easily understand my

unsaid words and the way you ignore

the world just to make time for me.

Yes, I feel so special and if it's love

then I am ready to confess

that I am deeply in love with you.

2. My Love for YOU

And see how my love will make you glow everyday.

You'll be the happiest soul as I'm ready to give my all to you.

You'll never feel judged, broken or sad.

I won't let any kind of negativity and problem touch you.

My words are heavy but my love is true,

No matter how tough the time is,

My heart will only beat for you.

3. I Am Possessive

Yes, I am a complicated person.

I don't like to express anything but I remember everything.

I like to notice things & this is both a beautiful and terrible thing because

I will always remember the way you smile since

I've watched it countless times.

I know little details about you that

you've forgotten you have told me because my mind doesn't let me forget

them. It's who I am.

On the flip side there's still me through all

of it - a person I think can't possibly be as interesting as you.

I am full of thoughts and feelings that

I don't know how to say out loud sometimes.

So, yes, I am a hard person to love because

I look at you in one way but myself in another.

4. Your Love Makes Me Feel Better

Yes I cry. Not because I want to gain

sympathy from you but I feel comfortable

enough to share my true feelings with you.

I know you won't make fun of me, instead

you'll make me understand that crying isn't

the solution, standing up whenever I fall is.

I cry in front of you because know you are

there to wipe my tears, to hug me tight and

to calm me down. I know I can trust you to

share every little thing with you, to put my

life completely naked in front of you.

I cry because I know you won't take advantage

of my vulnerability, instead you will give me

every ounce of love and advice to make me

feel that I am never alone as you are always

there with me to guide me and give me

all the support I need.

5. You Are My Soul

You're the person I can tell my secrets to,

The first person I want to talk to when I wake up,

and last person I want to talk to before I drift off to sleep.

When something good happens, you're the first person I want to tell.

When I'm troubled by something or if I get a bad news,

you're the one I go to for support.

But you're so much more to me than a friend

or someone who helps me in tough times,

you're the love of my life. You're my friend,

my lover, my comfort, and my strength.

I am so lucky to have you. And will always Love You <3

6. Men Needs Love Too

Men too get mood swings and need someone who can pamper them.

They too feel broken when their close one's hurt them.

They too want someone who can make them feel special.

Yes, they don't cry easily but that doesn't mean that things don't affect them.

They don't say, they don't show, they don't even confess their feelings towards someone.

Being a man is never so easy and being a gentleman is quite a tough job.

Not all the men are same.

Just because one man cheated on you please do not be judgmental about the whole men community.

They too deserve someone who can understand their unsaid emotions, give priority to their presence, heal their pain, pray for their happiness, read their mind and stay by their sides no matter what tomorrow brings.

7. How Much Do I Love You?

I Love You

Enough to fight for you and compromise for you.

Enough to miss you when we're apart, no matter what length of time it is and regardless of the long distance.

Enough to believe in our relationship, to stand by it through the worst of times and to have faith in us as a couple.

Enough to spend the rest of my life with you, be there for you when you need or want me.

I never ever want to leave you or to live without you. I love you this much.

8. You Care For Me

Time has made me realise, choosing you was one of the best decisions of my life

You make me believe in myself that I can do better.

You care for me like my parents

You don't just pamper and appreciate me but You respect and trust me (although sometimes you feel jealous but trust me, that's damn cute).

You complete me in every way.

Stay with me forever.

9. Isn't It Perfect?

I am weak, I am moody, I am crazy

but all these things are just for you because

you are the one for whom my heart beats,

you are the one in whose arms I want to spend my every night and start my
morning by kissing you.

You're the only one who knows what I was and what I am now. No one
knows me better than you

I love you and this is not temporary, it's for the whole life, your hands into
mine, our hearts beating for each other,

What can be more perfect than this?

10. I Trust You

The way you care about my every little thing makes me feel like I'm special to you,

the way you hold my hand or hug me makes me feel like I'm very close to your heart.

You call me hundred of times when I'm sick and guide me to take some of the most important decisions of my life which makes me feel like you care about me.

The way you get angry for not taking care of myself or behave like a joker to make me laugh, the way you call me your angry bird and the way you sleep on my lap makes me feel like home.

Yes, your presence makes me feel loved in a way that I've never felt before and

I feel proud and happy to call you mine because I know you'll never make me regret for loving you.

11. What I'd Lose For You

You're the only one who I wouldn't mind losing sleep for,

The only one who I can never get tired of talking to and

The only one who crosses my mind constantly throughout the day.

You're the only one who can make me smile without trying, bring down my mood without the intention and affect my emotions with every action of yours.

I can't explain with just words how much you mean to me but

You're the one I'm afraid of losing and the one I want to keep in my life

12. Yet I Lost You

I used to be the reason behind her smile once

I'm the person who hurts her the most now.

My presence used to be her best gift

She doesn't even want to see my face now.

My voice used to be a lullaby for her

Now it irritates her the most.

She wanted to hold my hand once

She left it in the middle of nowhere.

I was the person she wanted to spend her rest of life with,

Now I'm the person she doesn't want to spend a second with.

My love was everything for her once

That same love is a curse for her now.

Yes, people change and it hurts a lot when the person you loved the most doesn't want to be with you anymore.

I don't know what changed her but one thing I know for sure is, it broke in thousand pieces.

13. I Just Miss YOU

I know you'll never come back now and that hurts more when I think that I won't ever be able to hold your hand, hear your voice, hug you, kiss you, have food with you, laugh with you again.

It breaks my heart when I think that after few years you'll marry someone else and we won't be able to be together again. I can't tell you how much it makes me sad and cry. I don't know how to get you back. If I had one wish right now I could've asked the God for you. I loved you the most and now missing you the most. I don't know why did you leave but this is killing me.

14. I Am Attached To Her

Yes, I proposed her

Because I love her

Because I want to live with her

I want to die with her

Because I need her

I want to greet her

I want to fight with her

I want to play with her

Because I am a wanderer

She is my destination

And love is a road

By which I can achieve her

I don't want to hurt her

I don't want to hurt her feelings

Not just her body

I want to take all of her.

15. You Keep Me In YOU

I'll be in your heart,

I'll be in your mind,

Whenever you're rude,

Whenever you're kind.

I'll be in your past,

I'll be in your future,

I'll be your stumbles,

I'll be one of your tutor.

I'll be in your smile

I'll be in your tear,

I'll be your strength

I'll be you fear.

I'll be in your silence,

I'll be in your noise,

I'll be your peace,

I'll be your voice.

I'll be in your dates

I'll be in your life

I wanna make you mine

Will you be my wife?

16. You Are My Everything

Her smile

Is my life

Her eyes

Are world

Her hair

Are my veins

Her dress

Is my dignity

Her heart

Is my home

Her cheeks

Are my beats

Her lips

Are my drink.

She's my lifeline

She's my everything.

17. Guess I Can't Stop Loving You

Hey, I love you!!

I know, this is very old

There's nothing new

But I love you.

I love you.

I know, you don't care

And you don't believe either

But this is true

That I love you.

I know, your heart is full of pain

And your eyes have too much dew

But that's not the matter,

Because I love you.

I love you.

I know, the differences between us are many

And the chances of getting you are very few

But I don't care,

Because I seriously love you.

I love you.

Since I was just a kid

And will keep loving till the color

Of my blood changes to blue

I love you

And I'll always love you.

18. Who Are We Still Kidding?

We both knew better than anyone else that the fire once burnt our souls slowly started to die out.

Those dreams once we both shared slowly started to vanish and that those promises once made by us slowly started to break.

I wonder if you ever meant those words you once used to say so easily.

I guess, not all stories end with "happily ever after." Maybe ours was simply

not meant to be

I somehow work it out.

I thought we would somehow manage to grow old together but

I guess, I was wrong. thought we would always

Maybe it was over a long time ago.

19. Be With Someone Who Can..

1. Who can be loyal like a soldier and fight for you when it is needed.

2. Who can be deep at times like a write and writer long paragraphs and poems for you, on you.

3. Who can sing songs for you and make you fall asleep at nights by singing lullabies.

4. Who can see your beauty in any situation or condition just like a photographer does.

5. Who can make your life colorful by adding all the colors to your life just like a painter does.

6. Who can play different roles (guardian, boyfriend, bodyguard etc.) for you at different times just like an actor does.

7. Who can make you laugh when ever you feel tired and lonely. Just like a comedian does.

Love someone who can treat you as a beautiful and precious art of the God. That person will always adore you and never lose interest in you. You'll understand the meaning of true love because of that one person.

20. SHE is..

She is my road

She is my destination

She is my medicine

She is the pain

She is my poem

She is a tale

She is the sun

She is my rain

She is my prayer

She is the saint

She is my soul

She is my mate

She is a diamond

She is a pearl

She is my love

She is my dream girl.

(Waiting for my dream girl to come and complete me.)

21. Yes, It's ME

Right behind you

And I am not lying

My words are true

As much as the mountains are high

And the sky is blue

I got many people

But I talk to only few

When it came to my life

My heart chose you

I won't change ever

But everyday my love would be new

Till the last time of my life

My eyes wants your view

Where are you searching?

I live within you.

Three

1. I Quit

Dear Love,

Today I quit ,

I know I'll hurt you again after a period of time with a reality that I still love you and you will end up getting distracted just because of me. I know you are happy without me, and your happiness is what I wanted at the end. Its very hard for me to block you. Its just like keeping a mountain above my heart.

Ok fine no more words from my side again. You have a good memory to remember those time we spent together, the chats we had, names we gave to each other especially deciding name of our babies, and do you remember we even planned about our future together Dreams we saw were my motivation for life, and that first coffee date where I clicked your funny pics, you kissed me in the middle of a silent road under the cold sky, and those never ending casket hugst hugs. When it was time for me to leave you always stopped me by saying 'please dont go,Stay a little longer' and before I could say anything you kept your hands in my mouth and kissed above it. Aroma of your hair, Smell of that perfume.

Sorry sorry, No more words from my side Stay happy always. But remember I always loved You. even Now I love you Ok sorry again no more words. Wish you stopped me again from saying this things just like you did earlier.

Yours

Once everything.

2. You Make Me A Poet

The words I use

Use when we talk

Talks alot about me

Me and my love

Love that I've got for you

You who's in my heart

Heart that craves for your glance

Glance which makes me happy

Happy are days

Days where you're present

Present is what you're for me.

Me and my soul feel empty in your absence

Absence triggers a fear of losing

Losing myself and your love

A love which is so tender and worthy

Worthy enough to be careful about the fragile heart

Heart which races it's beats on hearing your name,

Name which never fails to remind me of the love games

Games like flames and fights which are solvable

Solvable even when love seems incapable

Incapable of holding the insecurities and mending the trust issues

Issues which need time to heal with utmost zeal

Zeal of beholding hands together, for today and forever.

Forever doesn't seem a lie now

Now is the time of cherishing eternity

Eternity which longs for our togetherness

Togetherness which has tangled love within,

Within this chaotic life and your mesmerising soul,

A soul like mine, now seems whole.

Whole you and your love made it

It doesn't crave for anything more

More are the beautiful moments these days

Days where I spend my time in your arms

Arms which feels like heaven

Heaven is what I see in your love

'Love' is what I call you now.

3. SOULMATE

Your soulmate is not someone that comes into your life peacefully. It changes your reality. It manages to revolutionize your world in a second. They stand by you through everything, understand your silence better than anyone else and are mentally and spiritually connected to you. The connection become so strong that you are drawn to them in a way you have never experienced before. A soulmate who is not afraid of your growth they do not need to close you off. The Soulmate does not complete you they inspire you to complete yourself. It doesn't care how you look and it doesn't care what you do And what you wear. A Soulmate is someone who help you to open your eyes come to terms that you are powerful beyond the measure and they are not afraid to inspire you until you finally see it too. They understand you in every way and on every level, which brings a sense of peace, calmness and happiness. That is Nearly how capable you are of becoming exactly who you have always wanted be.

4. Getting Weak

Sometimes there is this heaviness in our chest which we can't quite explain. Our throat gets dry and we feel like we have lost our voice. Our head gets heavy and all we want is to cry out loud. Things start to spin and dizziness takes over before we can even realize it. We want to escape this endless maze but it seems hopeless.

Darling, the pain that is piercing through your heart won't last long. You might feel short of breath but please do not stop breathing. My words might sound to you like they have once sounded to me but trust me, the sky is full of happiness.

5. Your Eyes

May be it was your long eye lashes or may be it was your mesmerizing wide eyes, may be it was both that were enchanting enough to capture my attention there for so long! To be honest, I got completely lost into depth of your eyes. I got this feeling by looking straight into your eyes that you're the one, the right one, the one they talk about in stories about true love, happy endings and fairytales. I got this instincts right away that you are definitely the one with whom I can share my happiness and sorrows, with whom I can share strengths and vulnerabilities, with whom I can share my dreams and desires, with whom I can share my body and soul, with whom I can share this lifetime and even my next ones.

Love, your eyes are no ordinary, they are heaven for me.

6. What Is Perfection?

Perfection is not muscular body and having those abs, it is your chubby red cheeks that I love to pull as I enjoy doing it and then we both giggle over this.

Perfection is not dyed hair and having flawless skin, it is your messy black hair and freckled skin that I love to touch and play with.

Perfection is not that particular english accent and knowing mutiple languages, it is your native sweet punjabi language that sound even more sweeter in your voice.

Perfection is not having clean shave face and using lots of beauty products, it is your not-so smooth not -so rough face and your beard that I like to run my fingers on.

Perfection is not having fancy expensive cars and wearing branded clothes, it is any of your vehicle and clothes you got through your own money earned by investing all of you in years of hardwork.

Perfection is not you always being so strong and not showing emotions just because you are a man, it is about being very honest about your emotions and showing your vulnerablities in front of me.

Perfection is not your dominant nature that you'll take me out and protect me everywhere, it is you encouraging me to be self-dependent and strong.

Perfection is not promising me to bring me moon and stars and buying me expensive gifts, it is taking out time for me to be always there for me no matter how busy your schedule is, trust me time is the most priceless gift.

Perfection is not offering me whole wide world and giving me an fairytale life, it is about being very realistic about hardships of life and building our own fairytale together.

Perfection is not getting both of us a safe grand place to live, it can be any kind of place to live as long as you allow me to jump into your arms as your arms are my first home and I feel safe there the most

7. *Love is Love*

Once you fall in love, you become a totally different person. The person whom you have fallen for becomes your top most priority. You crave to meet them. Their voice give you peace and their smile seems the most beautiful thing in the world. You feel safe in their arms and it's their presence that makes you feel complete. You start dreaming your life with them. On one hand love make you strongest while on the other, sometimes it make you weakest. Loving someone truly is the most divine feeling in the world. Once in life every one should feel what love actual is. And I am talking about love not about relationships. Love will always remain love no matter whether it's one sided or two sided..

LOVE IS LOVE.

8. *All I Want Is...*

Someone with whom I can cuddle.

Someone who can hug me from behind &

kisses my forehead before we go to sleep.

Someone who hugs me tight on bad days

and pulls me more close on cold nights.

One who understands my deep thoughts

& also makes fun of my lame jokes. One

with whom I can laugh & not mind crying.

Someone who knows how strong I am but

is there to help if I ever feel weak. One

who writes me cute little notes & knows

how much I like my coffee. Someone who

reads me stories & writes me poetries.

Someone who not only touches me or

My skin but one who touches my soul.

9. With You!

When I'm with you, I act differently. In a good way of course. I smile more and laugh more. I don't have to pretend everything is okay when it's really not

With you, I can drop the fake smile and put on a real one. I don't feel hurt and alone when I'm with you.

Instead, I feel safe and loved. You're easy to talk to, and you listen to me. I don't have to worry about holding back with you. I don't feel self conscious. I don't ever feel insecure or sad. You show me that you really do care, and you're not just pretending. I really appreciate your company, because with you I'm different. With you, I'm happy.

10. I'll Always Love You

I love you.. Please listen, I don't want someone else, I just want you. I want you during my good and bad times. I want you to be with me, holding my hand when everyone who said "I will be there for you" leaves me, and I can still see you & smile proudly. I know sometimes things are hard between us but I will tolerate it all just for you. Everytime you ask me, "If I'm tired of your weird behaviour?", I'll still say "No, I cant make promises to you about the moon and stars but atleast I can try to make you smile whenever I can. Don't ask me "Why I always want you and not anybody else?", it's hard to explain, no one can understand me better than you, no one can actually make me smile the whole day with those lovely texts. It's not always about saying "I love you to each other" but then whenever I see you sad it ruins my mood, those hugs which makes me feel better, I can't ever have it from someone else. Yeah I may find someone else but I just want you. So no matter what happens, remember "I'll always love you". I'm never ever going to leave you no matter what happens, U got it?

11. What Is Love?

Love is a slow process. You don't fall in love with someone overnight. The day after your first date, you nurture your bond. Like a seed needs to be watered slowly everyday, the bond needs to enfolded slowly with each passing day. You notice the highs and lows of the person and still choose to love them. You start liking their flaws, and all those little things which might be completely ordinary for them seem special to you. We often rush about our feelings at times and fail to understand that before actually going down on your knees and proposing her, think and understand whether the relationship is actually needed or not. It's not any game from which you can back out anytime, it's something which should be followed sincerely and responsibly. Because love indeed is a beautiful feeling, so before taking the next step give your heart ample amount of time to think over it.

12. No One Can Replace You

It's not easy to explain,

but if your love is true and pure

then that person's name will put a smile on your face,

that person's thoughts will make you happy,

their happiness will bring you happiness,

that very person's presence will make you feel complete,

their smile will bring a smile on your face,

that person's tears will bring tears into your eyes,

their success will make you proud,

their failure will make you feel failed too,

that person's smile, happiness and success will be the thing

that you will always crave for and that person will always reign on top of everyone in your heart, "a special place that no-one can ever be capable of replacing".

13. Will You?

Will you listen to my boring and nonsense talks?

Will you click my good pictures, always?

Will you hold me close and tight, whenever I will cry?

Will you share cheesier bites of pizzas with me?

Will you sing and dance with me in the rain?

Will you stay by my side during tough times?

Will you love me like no one else can ever love?

Will you keep all my secrets safe?

Will you always push me to be a better person?

Will you come to me, even after a huge fight?

Will you always support me in every aspect of life?

Will you be mine for the rest of my life?

14. It's Not Always The Way It Looks

You think they fall for your looks but they fall when you treat them like a little kid.

You think they want expensive gifts but chocolates, ice creams and flowers make them happiest.

You think they want account passwords but what they ask for is loyalty, even behind their backs.

They may turn moody, rude, dramatic sometimes but they just want someone who will listen to their nonsense.

They want to go on long night walks holding your hand on an empty road instead of going for long drives in your expensive car.

They want you to sing for them and dance in rain like nobody is watching.

They want you to hug them when they are sad and click their candids when they are the happiest.

They want you completely and want to be your favourite.

They want a future with the person they are in love with..

Dude, girls are damn complicated.

15. What If LOVE Is.....

If love is a religion then,

which God should I worship,

what prayers should I recite,

and how many candles should I light

inorder to lose all my hardships?

If love is a person then,

what does it look like,

is love really blind or

it's just the assumption

made by human psyche?

If love is a country then,

what language do its citizens speak,

do we pay with kisses there?

What are the rules to play fair

and what if someone commits a crime,

do they get a curse

of being single for lifetime?

If love is a season then,

what season will it be?

Will it be a rainy one

where we get drenched

without realising

that we're getting wet,

or will it be like summers

where the sun keeps shining,

giving us hope of a brighter life ahead?

I don't know what love is,

that's why I keep fantasizing about it

because when it approaches me,

I should know what it feels like

So that I don't confuse it with addiction, infatuation or it's other copycats,

So that I don't get played

in the name of love, all over again.

❧❧❧

16. The Moment I Fell In Love With You

When I look back to that

beautiful day,

the short eye contact

with you still feels like forever.

I was so happy,

that I could feel alive.

the moment I could say,

that everything feels like a miracle.

I wonder, if maybe

your each step towards me

is difficult for you,

I'll make sure that

on the count of three

we'll walk together.

In the absence of you,

my mind is shattered

until we get it together.

You kept on saying,

I kept on listening,

the story ended

but the path of my life mended.

Even if our paths are away from

each other, but darling

just standing under the same sky

would make me happy.

And if the sky falls down

or the ground sinks under the earth,

the breeze which you'll feel for the last moment,

is the love for you by me.....

17. She Is Mine

She is mine

A little messy

A little crazy

But that's fine

Because she is mine.

Yes, she is mine.

Very talkative

Always angry

But that's fine

Because she is mine.

She makes me shine

She drives me crazy like a wine

But that's fine

Because she is mine.

She is naughty

She is busy

She doesn't have time

But that's fine

Because she is mine.

She is my word

She is my poem

She is my rhyme

Because she is just mine

And she will always be mine....

18. Yours, Broken Hearted

To the one who couldn't love me back,

Before I begin, I want to blurt out that one question which my heart had asked me for around a thousand times since you rejected me; was there a fault in our stars or a fault within me? Hey wait! calm down, I neither want to play blame games nor I want to investigate why things didn't work out like a fairytale between us. A part of me feels glad to have known of your false hopes at the earliest, but another part of me is pleading for a miracle which would have an effect of bringing us together. People often curse love to be a much disastrous emotion yet the truth is, love is the most blissful feeling when cultured around the right person and drastic, around the wrong person. and the biggest trouble is for those broken hearts, who look up to someone with a ray of new hope to mend their incomplete souls by mingling in the tunes of one-sided love? After my first heartbreak, I was completely done with relationships, though the torn apart pieces of my heart succeeded to wound me from within upon seeing the couples happy together, still my senses want to scream at every human who cried buckets for the by gones of their beloved who in reality never actually cared for them. Confessing my feelings to you was never in my wishlist because I was aware that I couldn't bear the pain of rejection, since I wasn't ready anyway to lose the beautiful bond we share. But in the peer pressure I ended up spilling my love for you over a few shots of tequila without knowing that even the cure for the pain of your rejection will be alcohol. I still love you, perhaps half-heartedly because the rest half of my soul is trying to heal, since I hate witnessing myself in a vulnerable condition pleading for someone's attention. You were, are and will always be important to me, I really wish that you find your significant other soon and never break her from within, the way you did with me -

Yours,

Broken Hearted

19. Nobody Like You

You might make me cry but nobody

can make me smile like you do.

You annoy me like hell but nobody

can make me blush like you do.

You fight with me sometimes but

noone takes care of me like you do.

Although sometimes I feel

I should let you go,

yet I feel so lost without you.

Nothing is same without you.

Nothing makes sense.

But when you are there with me,

everything is at peace.

I may feel like killing you when we argue,

but when we get along, it feels perfect.

Yes, with you, I'm imperfectly perfect.

20. I Am Proud Of Being With You

Baby,

You made me capable,

Told me I was brave,

Made me who I am Today,

Loved and cared for me.

You made me feel special,

Told me I wasn't silly,

You encouraged me to fight,

And gave me inspiration.

You assured me I wasn't alone,

And told me you were there for me.

When I cried,

You made me laugh.

You hugged me when I was sad,

Told me I wasn't at all bad.

You always gave me ears,

And never let me down.

I could share everything with you,

You consoled me.

You comforted me in my bad,

You gave me the strength I never had

All I want to say to you is

I Love You So Much...

21. Dating The Right Girl

Date the girl whose hair is a total mess and steals your t-shirts, who kisses you in front of boys who look at her admiringly.

Date the girl who wants to dance in the rain with you and make tea for you and make you laugh hard.

Date the girl who knows you that she can tell something is wrong just by looking at you.

Date the girl who will wrap her arms around you for no reason and pay attention when you talk about the things you love even if she does not love them herself.

Date the girl who is not able to sleep till she makes up your sad mood & makes you smile.

Yeah, date that girl.!!

Four

1. Men Are Humans Too

"Men don't cry", are the words that

every crying young boy would hear.

What are you supposed to do then,

when you're in sadness and despair?

Many men never dare to say,

if their favourite colour is pink.

As from childhood, most of their possessions resemble to blue ink.

Sitting idle at home,

they're marked dumb and unemployed.

But by thinking about their salary scale,

the whole society gets annoyed.

All these high expectations

from the family and the society,

it literally kills them from inside,

yet they never show any anxiety outside.

They must be strong enough, as they're

the shoulder for everyone to lean on,

they must be a shield for the family,

yet by striving hard all alone.

By being a man,

they must sacrifice their dreams,

only to look after their family,

even if costs to ignore their inner screams.

And when a baby is born,

"It's a boy ", can be heard in a happy voice.

So the question to all men would be,

Being a man, is it that pleasing to rejoice?

2. Hey Love,

Hey listen,

I don't know

how to confess

everything in front you,

but I'll have to now

as it has become

difficult for me

to live without you.

I don't know whether

it's the right time or not,

it's the right decision or not

but I'll have to do it.

I'll have to tell you

about my feelings for you

which keep on increasing

with every conversation,

I'll have to say it out..

When we talked

for the very first time,

we were just strangers

who texted each other

only because of

professional reasons,

but as we kept talking

and started knowing each other,

it became difficult for me

to stop my heart,

which was falling for you.

Your purity,

your kindness

and your soulful talks

made me feel like

my heart was meant

to be in love with you.

.

The way you opened up

and made me comfortable

was something very new for me,

as no one in the past could do that

and I was called a rude person

by everyone but not by you,

you understood the real me

and saw a sweet child within me

which no one else ever did.

You are not like others,

you're very different

and precious too.

It seems like you know me

since a long time

and all these which seem

strange aren't actually new.

.

I don't know how you feel,

I don't how you'll react,

whether you'll slap me

or you'll delete my contact.

But i'll have to tell you

that how I fell for you,

because rejection is bad

but regret is worst of all.

So listen carefully now

I have something to say;

I love you my darling

not till the moon and back

but to the level where

I can understand you

and feel you totally.

Where insecurity,

jealousy and doubts

are just mere words,

my love will stay strong

till the time I'm on this earth

and maybe, after that too.

3. To The Girl Who Feels Like Love

I don't know if at all someday, somewhere, sometime, someone will hold
your hand in Winter and look into your eyes to tell you, "Khoobsurat hai
har vo lamha, jinme teri muskurahat khil khilati hai" ("All those moments
are beautiful in which your smile blossoms.") Cheesy? Sorry, but that's how
it works. I remember this one time when one of my was crying in the
summer. I ask her what happened and she says, "You can't make people love
you back but you can't stop loving them at the same time" and I just
couldn't do much but sit beside her and think of you. I do feel like telling
you how madly I want to hug you and whisper in your ears all those songs
you love. The clock in my bedroom sometimes chimes and it's almost
unavoidable to hear your name in it. I'm a broken man, who counts stars

sitting alone on roof and just wants the night to stay a little longer for I fear to see a morning with this hollow chest that can't feel the warmth of sunshine. But, somehow, when I see you smile with the curves of your lips forming soft wrinkles around your eyes, I just feel a tinge of completion around me. And then, here's where all of it ends. After everything that's said and done, I'm not the home that can shelter your gorgeous heart. But, I just want to tell you, for once, I want to hold you in my arms and believe that I'm still allowed to be loved. If at all someday you read this, just know that I can't bring you the moon, but I'll show you a mirror, ask you to smile and that's where my moon lives. That's where it always will be.

4. For Me You Are Way More Beautiful Than Anyone Else

There's this beautiful girl,

not just any normal girl

when I see the glitter in her eyes,

I feel like kissing her until time flies.

She can get anyone's attention,

yet she loves it convention

she lives far away from home,

and is hard like a pome.

All the beautiful moment we shared together,

how I long to be with her forever.

She loves cuteness all around,

all I wish to see her being crowned..

she doesn't need a short dress and a huge makeup,

a little eyeliner and a lipgloss is enough.

Happiness can't be brought she somehow manages to get it

from the things she shops.

I'm not the perfection In her world,

but she loves the imperfections in her perfect world.

After all I wish,

She could see the angel I see,

When she reads my words with glee

In my world of nothingness,

She is my everything.

There's this beautiful girl,

She will always be the only girl.

5. Do You Believe In LOVE?

Well, love isn't a myth or a fact that you get to choose if you want to believe in it or not. Love is a feeling and you really don't have the power to control it. Maybe you can pretend that you don't believe in love anymore and that, you don't even believe in its existence. But then, deep down we all crave to find the love which we read about, watch and feel around us. Love has a magic and power within it that forces you to believe over it's existance and that it has the power of healing even the deepest of scars, way too easily. All you need to do is just hang on there and wait, wait for that one soul to magically enter in your life and fill it with immense happiness, the soul whose strings would get entangled with yours and then, you'd be proudly able to say that yes, I do believe in the magic of love.

6. Have You Ever Been So Close To Someone, That It Shattered You Completely?

We often read or hear this and let go off, but do we realise that each one of us faces this at some or the other point of time in life. We give our one thousand percent to someone and they just give their 10 or maybe 20 percent efforts at maximum and leave us easily saying that, "Your love is toxic for me" or "You expect a lot from me, which I can't give you in return" or "You're just insensitive and naive." These all words kill us from inside and the wounds they cause don't end easily, they create a chain just like a reaction which goes on and on creating a reaction which is neither acidic nor basic but it just becomes toxic and more toxic with the passage of time. They leave and go so far that we become incapable of reaching out to them, we miss them and their memories, the moments that we shared with them, the places that we went with them, the things that we did with them. They just try to prove that you're an emotional fool and they're always right in everything, they try to make you feel like a loser or someone who is incapable of handling their relations properly. All these things hurt you and the pain which you feel is much more than any physical pain, the pain that's hard to express, the pain that doesn't hurt you anywhere but directly in your heart and you feel so numb that your world seems to be breaking apart, everything seems to be going away, you just feel lost and like a loser who isn't ready to move forward in life or do anything, you just cry litres of tears and vent your heart out..

7. *You Need Courage To Be In Love*

Love is like a glass jar

Sitting on the table

Next to me,

Which I am afraid to hold in my hands,

As I may drop it on the floor,

And the broken pieces

Will pierce my skin

And make me bleed.

I have been a little soldier

All this while,

Holding guns and missiles,

Protecting the walls

And the shores.

T have been at war

With myself

Since ages,

But it takes much more Courage

To be in love

Than it does for the war

Now, my soul is tired

And my skin is bruised,

I am scared

To love again

But I gather all the courage

To fall in love

With all my flaws

Because if I can't love myself

How can I expect

Someone else to be in love with me....

8. To The One I Love Way Too Much.

It's You, who makes me "me". You are not just a part of my life, you are my most important chapter. I'm so perfect at doing mistakes. I'm so focused on getting disturbed. I'm so brilliant at judging folks. I'm so smart to believe those lies. But, it's you who brought me here. It's you who makes me feel secured. It's you who corrects me everytime I do mistakes. Anything I can do good is all because of you. If there's anything that's going good, going great, its Us. I know many times I've been mad at you. There are many times that you can find the best way to get over. But you direct me, you correct me, you make me perfect.

I've never been so frustrated, as I see you getting depressed.

I've never been so happy, as I am after seeing you smile.

I've never been so annoyed, as I see to getting irritated.

I've never been so secured, as I am when next to you.

And I know that no matter how many letters I write to you it won't be enough anytime. And I promise that I won't ever let you down anytime. I've never been so emotional, as I get seeing your emotions. It's YOU.

9. To The Girl Who Made Me Believe In Love Again

To the girl who made me believe in love again,

It's tough to love someone again after a breakup, to have the same amount of trust and to also convince your heart that this love would stay. The concept of forevers seem misleading after heartbreaks, but maybe it opens the floodgates for a type of love which you have always deserved to possess. Despite being in the same class as mine,l was always hesitant to approach you first due to shy nature. That day when you approached my seat the long lost butterflies appeared again in my stomach. You were a different kind of beautiful. Everything seemed perfect about you. You took me to places not physically but mentally which I could never imagine of. Your name had spontaneity, excitement, joy. It all made sense now. To all the loneliness I encompassed myself in after my first love failure, you as a sweet magician disappeared everything away in a flash. My life was never perfect but I thank you for making it a little less lonely. I'm glad to have your laughter as my favourite sound, your smile as my favourite masterpiece. I'm glad that my heart chose you. And I'll choose you, over and over again. I don't know what you feel about me. I'm not an astrologer who can predict that we'll go on a honeymoon in the future. I don't know whether I'm the one you will choose to hold your hand but one thing I'm certain of is whatever you face in your life, we are going to face it together. Whether they are the struggles, happiness or any other problems, you'll always have my back. "If we go down then we go down together, We'll get away with everything, Let's show them we are better" Maybe or maybe not our love would last forever, but let's assure ourselves that till whenever it lasts, it's the best moment of our lives.

From,

The one who craves only for your presence.

10. Have You Ever Been The Reason?

Have you ever been the reason,

of making someone's cheeks red

and felt so special?

Have you ever been the reason,

of someone's good times

and felt so special?

Have you ever been the reason,

of someone's private conversation in their heads

and felt so special?

Have you ever been the reason,

of someone's light in a dark night

and felt so special?

Have you ever been the reason,

of making someone's eyes stare at you

and felt so special?

Have you ever been the reason,

of someone's sleepless nights

and felt so special?

Have you ever been the reason,

of making someone smile all the time

and felt so special?

Have you ever been the reason,

of someone's never ending dreams

and felt special?

Indeed, it feels so special to be a part of these beautiful experiences..

11. Two Fighters

Two lovers,

who loved each other

more than anything

were lost in a world

of people having

sick mentality

and a lot of hatred.

They became rebels,

they became crazy,

fighting for each other

as they didn't want

to lose each other

at any cost,

in any situation.

Not knowing

what to do,

how to do and

where to go,

they kept fighting

for the person they loved

and for the love

which they wanted to have forever.

They were doing every

possible thing for it.

The efforts they made

to save their relationship

proved that true love

still exists.

The thought of losing

their partner made them

strong and it was

enough for them

to keep fighting

till their last breath.

They were separated,

they were beaten,

they were insulted,

but it didn't matter

as the only thing

they had within

was the never ending love.

They fought,

they fought very hard

and left no other option

for this society

other than accepting

their love;

the tears they had

in their eyes were

not because they won

but because they were

together again,

stronger than earlier,

with more feelings for each other,

with more craze

and with more purity.

It was not their win,

but the success of their love

and whenever

tue love will face

difficulties in future,

the lovers will always

remember them

and thank them

as their story will become

immortal and it will give

power to the lovers,

so that they can stand

and fight for their love too.

$$\text{❧❧❧}$$

12. *When I Look At You!!*

V. When I look at you,

I see a dysfunctional me

slowly trying to stay calm,

composed yet happily lost

in your eyes, dancing,

smiling, singing Usher's "My Boo"..

iv. When I look at you,

I see answers to those

3 questions I repeat to myself

every single morning.

What's there today?

How will I survive?

Why wake up?

iii. When I look at you,

I fall into the abyss,

a bottomless pit in hell,

but i see a hand holding mine

and pulling me up

till heaven shows up.

ii. When i look at you,

I see a wildflower blooming

from everything inside of me

that's fissured,

flawed and damaged,

i. When I look at you,

I actually see all my poetry,

each metaphor I craft,

falling short of words.

I see a dream that's

better than this life,

And a life that going to be

better than this dream.

13. *This One Is For Your Bestfriend!*

Whenever I ran out of words,

you completed me in a while.

Whenever I felt low,

you were always there to bring a smile.

When I forgot my textbook,

you acted as if you did too.

You were there throughout,

even if we had different goals to pursue.

Without talking to you,

my day feels incomplete.

Every time I miss you,

I long for those days to repeat.

You picked me up

every single time I fell.

At the end of the day,

you made sure that I'm all well.

I hope you don't feel anything,

because I never express.

This is all that I can dedicate,

to the 'bestest' person I guess.

Crushes changed

and so did valentines.

But my dear best friend,

not even the fights or the distance could make our friendship end..

14. To The One Who Felt Like "FOREVER"

Watching you smile beside me, like you're really living the life I dreamt of building one for us, felt more than just reality. Seeing you become depressed, on days I was going rough made me realise for a long time, that you feel what I go through. Holding your hand silently when no-one's watching, making you blush like a kid, had me believe in the fact that you are equally wanting to stay. Letting you make the little changes in my monotonously vague life, while you made sure it never affected me too much, kept me thinking that you understand what I want. Talking to you for hours, and sometimes maybe, just seconds that feel enough to lift up my mood, told me again and again that you will be the jukebox of my life, forever. Making things complicated, arguing for silly what-abouts, figuring out each other's flaws, but then going back to where we settled down with an "I love you" each, made me feel you are just the one right decision I ever took in my life. I can keep on writing about things that say me you weren't the one who would quit. Give up. Walk away. Because you made me re-read the lines that said how People who understand true love too exist, and they who stick to each other no matter what, set examples for what forever may feel like to the world. You felt the same. Like forever. But then, I also remember how you used to love tales from movies or series, where often,

Heer-Ranjha,

Romeo-Juliet,

loved unconditionally but never made it to the living' forever mark. I can rest myself assured that we were one of them, who loved, lived, but couldn't end up right.

But was our love unconditional too?

Was your love one of those?

Were you actually aiming for a forever, with me?

-- Wanting a response to a letter I'll never send.

15. DREAM REWIND

When at eighty,

I saw you smiling

for the last time

it felt as if the sun

had lost a bit of

its glory and

for every crinkle that carried a memory;

a grey hair stood out

and told a

different story.

.

When at seventy

you gifted me a watch,

I never knew that it was us

who were running

out of time,

you see our lives had

become a full circle;

and I was the

tangent to your circumference -

separating us

would be a crime.

.

When at sixty-five

you were diagnosed

with cancer,

I wept like a child

who had lost

his favorite toy

but you had the

strength to keep us

both going;

you were my savior,

my pride and my joy.

.

When at fifty

we renewed our vows,

you looked like a

sunflower in full bloom

and as gold glittered

in your eyes

and heart;

once again, I became

the lucky groom.

·

When at forty-five

we became grandparents,

it felt surreal

to have come this far

and as I looked

at our family portrait;

I thought of the first

night we met -

at that tiny old bar.

·

When at thirty

we had a huge quarrel,

you slept in the

room on the next floor

but even when I

behaved at my worst;

you slid me food from under the door.

.

When at twenty-five

we brought a lily

into this world,

I saw the

metamorphosis

happening overnight

you were a fighter,

a protector and a mother;

she was the moon

to your sun - always shining bright.

.

When at eighteen,

I saw you smile

for the first time,

it felt as if the planets

in my ecosystem

had aligned,

perfect orbits that

brought me to you;

and stars that

glittered as our constellations

intertwined.

16. WORTH

He'll call just to hear your voice.

If he wants you he'll show it.

If he has a thought about you,

it will come out of his mouth.

If you are on his mind non stop,

he will do anything he can just to see you.

If he truly likes you,

he won't let anything get in the way

and fight back just to keep you in his arms.

If not, he is not worth your time

because you are obviously not worth his.

17. I'll Always

I'll choose you even when you make me mad

My love for you will not fade simply because we are angry.

I know we will fight, we will be frustrated, we will not talk to each other for
hours or days.

Still, I'll prefer to fight every battle of life and love only with you because

you are the one who has changed my life for better.

I know your anger is justified because you care for me.

I will always choose you and keep choosing you, every single day,

because I Love You and will continue to love you even in the bad days that
are ahead of us.

18. I Deserve The HATE

Sitting on the roof top

I was thinking about stuffs;

the past stories

and the things which will come into my cup,

a bit stressed,

a little lost,

I was trying to figure out

the things which matter to me the most.

I was still thinking,

when suddenly the weather changed,

It wasn't predicted

but as the unpredicted rain

kissed the earth;

it healed all the wounds

which were hidden in my heart.

The rain drops fell on the screen,

clearing the dust away

and making it green.

And with that,

water droplets fell from my eyes,

reminiscing the old days,

all the fights and the goodbyes.

I won't stop them

as I want them to flow out of my eyes,

making my soul feel light,

so that I can enjoy my day

and sleep peacefully at night.

I want everything,

every pain and every sorrow,

to come out through my eyes

in the form of tears.

I want this rain

to clean my heart,

my soul and my mind,

as I've a lot to explore

and I've a lot to find.

I am feeling each and every drop of water

falling from the sky,

touching my face,

as they are asking me to let go

all the harmful elements

and be ready to work

for the things which really matter,

they are asking me

to give my best shot for my dreams

which will bring me glory

and I'll be remembered

as an example of dedication,

hard work and live forever

in the stories.

Rain drops ask me for everything,

they ask me to reach the heights

as they don't want me to fall like them, ever.

19. Soul Bonding

We fight, sometimes you're right and

sometimes I'm right but the thing is,

does that really matter?

Can those small fights really kill our love?

No, it can't because only our minds and

mouth fights with each other not our

hearts and souls. We will be together as

long as our hearts are together and believe

me it is almost impossible to break that heart

to heart or soul to soul bonding. That is why

I don't fear losing you after any fight. I know

we'll be okay within hours and

will keep loving each other till the last...

20. Please Stay By My Side

You literally mean the world to me. I love you

beyond belief because you keep me happy

every day. I am the luckiest boy knowing that

I have you! I can't believe that we've come this

far and it makes me so grateful having you by

my side all the time. I miss you every second

when I'm not with you & I literally appreciate

everything you do for me! You're the sweetest,

most supportive, caring and hilarious person

I've ever met! All the memories we've had so

far have been a bliss and there are many more

to come. You make me laugh non stop. I can

always trust you. I would do anything just to

be with you, please do not ever leave

the hold of my hand..

21. Hey Love

Hey love,

You made me freeze

Stay with me till the end

Will you do so please?

Hey love,

You made me fall for you

The feeling I got today

Was extraordinary and very new.

Hey love,

CanI make you mine?

We'll be lovers for life

And partners in every crime.

Hey love,

Can I get your time?

I want to write poetries on you

I want to make you my rhyme.

Hey love,

You're prettier than my words

I'll love you more than anyone

Living on this earth.

Five

1. We Are Family

We don't talk much over calls,

Or text each other a lot,

and we meet after long breaks or months.

But whenever we meet,

we meet with the same

intensity and love,

it's been months

since we're together,

putting each other

in problems and

taking out of it.

We never left hands,

Which we'd held months ago

and are still fulfilling

all the promises.

We fight,

We abuse,

We become rude,

but we never betray,

We never lie

and we always stand

when any of us is in trouble.

There have been days

when we had serious fights

and it almost felt like

everything is gone,

but we always came back

with a stronger bond.

We still call each other

either by using the name

or by Nickname.

We tease each other

by shouting funny names.

We do crazy stuffs

and walk out of our houses,

for vacation without

even deciding the destination.

We drink sometimes

and keep reminding

the love we have

for each other and

how much this relationship

means to us.

We also plan to have

our children

in the near future.

We go to each other's house

and enter their kitchen

without any permission

and eat whatever we find there.

It's been more than months

since we're together,

tied with a strong bond

of friendship and we do

everything to insult

each other but still

we respect, care for

and love each other.

We're not friends anymore,

we've become a family now....

2. How Should We Start?

Where do I start from?

How should I start?

The story of us I mean

What kind of story it is?

Is it the story of the lasting

Hours you wasted on hopes of me?

Or is it simply a story of

My ignorance for accepting

Something so beautiful I can't

Begin to understand?

Did you ever resent me?

No?

Why not?

You should have.

You ought to have.

But if you did than

It wouldn't have been love,

That's what they say,

And I say fuck them.

What do they know about love?

Or wait or ignorance,

What do I know about any of?

You and I

Us and them

We are all simply characters

Actors, playing a part,

Who decides which part to play tho?

How does one decides?

What is the story?

Whose story it is?

Is it mine?

The story of being lost in ignorance,

Is it yours?

The story of endless wait,

Is it theirs?

The story that knows not

Where to end, when to begin

Are you playing a part in mine?

Am I playing a part in yours?

Are we each others stories?

Why do then they want to write it?

Why do they insist on coloring

Our skies blue, why can't they be orange?

Why do they ask you to smile

When they fuck everything up?

Why do they ask me to slow down

When I haven't even started yet?

If it's our story then

Why do they get 98 out of 100 pages?

Why can't we get atleast 68 of them?

Seriously, whose story it is?

If it's yours why do your pages

Knows my name better than yours?

If it's mine why do every date

Accounts to your presence?

Whose story it is?

Is it yours?

Is it mine?

Is it ours?

Do we have a story for us?

Is there any us?

If not than what are we?

Why are we?

If not to belong together,

If not to write a story,

If not to be a story,

Where do you think

We should start from?

How should we start?

3. I Love You Because..

I love you.

I love you because you actually put effort into me.

I love you because nobody has ever given me the love that you have given

me and

you are the only one that could ever love me this way.

I love you because you always make me feel that I am worth something

I love you because you have a nurturing nature and you take care of me.

I love you because you made me smile when I almost forgotten how to.

I love you because you have a huge and honest heart.

I love you and everything little detail about you.

I love you because you are simply you.

4. See You Again

When I see you again,

Will it be in the same way as before?

With your hands accidentally touching mine

and your touch reaching my heart's core.

With me asking the winds about you

and they saying that they've no clue..

When I see you again,

Will it be the same way like before?

With me thinking what's going in your mind

Whenever your eyes seem to cross mine.

With you always coming in my dreams

and waking me up by your eye's gleam.

When I see you again,

Will it be the same way like before?

Where just a 'Hi' from you would make my day

and my heart would play your voice even when I don't say.

With both of us turning old together

and instead of memories we'd behold love for one another.

When I see you again,

Will it be the same way like before?

With our bodies getting buried together

and without getting worried, we'd lay next to each other

5. What Is LOVE?

Love finds funny ways to tell you that it never left,

it hides along the curbs of the roads

you walk every day

holding a placard, "Lost love. It will find you".

It sits besides you in cab rides

engaging in awkward small talk,

it's in conversations over coffee

in old cafes on forgotten streets,

it's in the laughter of strangers shared over a cheesy joke

or the blush of lovers as they paint the sky red,

it follows you on your way back home,

it's the sound of a phone call

or the ping of an expected text,

it's the smile that comes after that.

Love hides in shared silences,

it waits next to your unread books

and turns pages of a story that could've been,

it's the music that plays in shared earphones,

it's the sound of tangled heartbeats,

it dwells near bouquet shops

and waits for lovers to pick roses for someone they wish to

live a forever with,

or maybe for someone who couldn't be more than a dream,

it stands a few feet away from you

every time that you talk to someone new

only waiting for you to give in once again,

but you don't,

and so it goes.

Anyway,

when you try to run from love

it starts appearing in things you see everyday,

you see it in a couple standing in a crowded train not aware of

the things around them,

love hides behind newspapers and sneaks glances at you

when you're not looking,

it waits in a boakstore with your favourite book in hand

hoping to have a conversation that would lead to a forever

after,

it waits,

patiently,

longingly,

for another chance,

it sits on the outside looking in,

it hides in familiar scents and forgotten words,

it's in shared interests and benign smiles,

You see,

you can't run from it,

because even though you threw it out,

love would always find a way to you again,

and you can never say no.

6. Letter To Heart

Dear Heart,

I am writing this to you with utmost greif and lament over multiple heartbreaks and betrayals. I should have listened to you when you'd screamed and cried, trying to tell me not to trust anyone in this fake world.

But, I always denied. My brain had another story to tell. A tale that was too convincing for me get close to others. You urged me to maintain distance from a few, you frowned in pain. But here I was standing like a fool, busy doing what my brain was asking me to do. I know you have suffered a lot. The pain that you got can never lessen just with a simple word " sorry ". I've left you in a fragile state now and I'm the reason for your happiness. After breaking down for several times now, when I don't have the courage to love again or get close to someone. I can understand what you must be going through. But, today I choose to collect all the precious peices of you which are scattered because of me and I wish to mend your agony. I want you to re live happily all over again. I want you to know that I have understood that there is no one real in this world except you, because you've been there with me since the day I opened my eyes in this world and I know you will be there with me until eternity supporting me in all my endeavors. My heart, it's time for you to bloom again with happiness because I promise to keep you safe with me now rather than giving you away in the hands of those people who would hurt you. Let's rejoice our life again and live with each other until eternity.

From,

The one who owes you until eternity.

7. *So In LOVE*

It isn't easy being so in love with you and

not being able to see you every day.

There are times when I'd give anything just

to be able to gaze into your eyes or hold you

in my arms, even if it's for just a few minutes.

I always feel incomplete, like a part of me is

missing, when we're not together. I know that

right now this is the way things have to be,

but that doesn't make it any easier to bear.

Every day without you reminds me of the joy

you add to my life. So always remember that

I'm thinking of you and counting every minute

until we're together yet again.

I Love You!

8. Dear Love

It's been quite a while since I last wrote to you.

I know we are far apart but our distances are held together by our hearts.

I know we don't meet a lot but your name forever revolves in my thoughts.

I do miss you but your memories never make me cry.

I look at your pictures and this makes my time to fly.

Dear Love, I know that

I don't have you here but your very essence has always been my strength.

Our distance keeps us closer and these miles have built us better.

Together we've fought for each other with each other.

You have my soul and I have yours, let's

keep it safe and our relationship to be pure.

Dear Love, I Love you to the rest and forever....

9. Reality Of 'RELATIONSHIPS'

A relationship is not just dreaming about a

fairy tale. It's about facing reality & supporting

each other in every phase. Several hardships

may come but it's our responsibility to hold

each other's hand and overcome them. Many

a times, destiny tests us but we must never

blame each other. Instead, we should share

everything with each other to come up with

a perfect solution.

Always remember, silence ruins a matter more

than speaking does. It creates unnecessary

misunderstandings. True love is not about

pushing each other away in worst phases but

it's about being on each other's side and

facing every situation together.

10. Without You

To the irreplaceable person of my life

I don't know what to say much,

it's just that everything is empty without you.

It's just that even the most favourite place

of ours seem annoying to me without you.

It's just that my smile lacks happiness without you,

Neither yours nor mine mistakes reduces

your value in my heart.

It's just that my life is incomplete without you.

11. Phases Of Love

In all my good and bad phases, morning and night

wishes, voice calls and video chats, you're mine and

will always be mine. I'll never let you go at any cost.

I'll do whatever I can to make our relationship turn

successful. I'll give my everything to keep you and

to make us last forever. I only hope that this bond

of ours gets stronger with time. I'll not let a tear fall

down your cheeks and even if they fall, I'll not sleep

until a bright smile flashes on your face again. I look

forward to spending my lifetime of happiness with you.

I Love You.

12. I Can't Lose You

You're the only one who I wouldn't mind

losing sleep for, the only one who I can

never get tired of talking to and the only one

who crosses my mind constantly throughout the day.

You're the only one who can make

me smile without trying, bring down my mood

without the intention and affect my emotions

with every action of yours.

I can't explain with just words how much you mean to me but

you're the one I'm afraid of losing and the one I want to keep in my life.

13. Presence Of Love

The way you care about my every little thing

makes me feel like I'm special to you, the way

you hold my hand or hug me makes me feel

like I'm very close to your heart. You call me

hundred of times when I'm sick and guide me

to take some of the most important decisions

of my life which makes me feel like you care

about me. The way you get angry for not taking

care of myself or behave like a joker to make

me laugh, the way you call me your angry bird

and the way you sleep on my lap makes me feel

like home. Yes, your presence makes me feel

loved in a way that I've never felt before and

I feel proud and happy to call you mine because

I know you'll never make me regret for loving you.

14. You Make Me Strong

I am weak, I am moody, I am crazy

but all these things are just for you

because you are the one for whom

my heart beats, you are the one in

whose arms I want to spend my

every night and start my morning

by kissing you. You're the only one

who knows what I was and what I

am now. No one knows me better than you

I love you and this is not temporary,

it's for the whole life,

your hands into mine, our hearts

beating for each other, what can

be more perfect than this?

15. For *A SPECIAL FRIEND.*

Sometimes all you need in life is one special friend,

someone who slaps the truth on your

face and makes you believe that even the

worst of you will be replaced by something better.

Someone who cheers you up on days

that you can't even be proud of yourself,

someone who urges you to strive and be the

best version of yourself. This one person who

always stays true to you no matter what

comes and they always stand by you through

the worst storms and the darkest times of your life.

And no matter what strikes you,

they will always have the time to help you

overcome your failures. Sometimes all you

need in life is a best friend who will always

walk with you no matter how tough life gets.

16. Best Decision

Time has made me realise, choosing

you was one of the best decisions of

my life You make me believe in myself

that I can do better. You care for me like

my parents You don't just pamper and

appreciate me but You respect and

trust me (although sometimes you feel

jealous but trust me, that's damn cute).

You complete me in every way.

Stay with me forever....

17. Tough Times

I Love You

Enough to fight for you and compromise for you.

Enough to miss you when we're apart,

no matter what length of time it is

and regardless of the long distance.

Enough to believe in our relationship,

to stand by it through the worst of times and

to have faith in us as a couple.

Enough to spend the rest of my life with you, be there for you when you need or want me.

I never ever want to leave you or to live without you. I love you this much........

18. Dear Favourite Person

You are the person who never lets me face

any difficulties alone, the person who stands

by my side no matter what.

You are that person who loves me without

any conditions, the person who gives respect

not only to me but also to everyone.

You are the person by whom I get inspired,

the person who not only forgives my mistakes

but also teaches me to learn something from them.

You are that person who comes after me when

I try to go away from you and the person

who looks damn cute while smiling.

You are that person who looks after me even

when I deny to look, the person because of

whom I started believing that good people

do exist in this world.

You are the person whom I never want to lose,

you are the person who never gets bored of me.

You are the reason of my biggest smile. You are

my bestfriend, my family and love for lifetime

which will always remain constant till the rest

of my life.

19. If We Date

I won't give you a forever,

rather than that

'll give you a happy living ever,

I'll take you to a place

where happiness comes from.

I will set you free

to stay who you want to be,

morning kisses and cuddles

are common,

I'll take you to morning drives,

I will lock myself in your eyes,

and fingers in your hair.

Somedays,

I'll cook for you

before you wake up

and sun kisses you

through the window,

I will kiss your forehead

and let you feel,

how much I love you.

During rains,

I won't let you only

get wet in it,

I will make you enjoy it,

along with aroma of clay.

On dark nights,

I will hold your hands

and make you fight through

your worst nightmares,

I will teach you to live in my absence,

I will secure you pensively,

as well as palpably,

surprise with dates,

locking you in my arms,

let you steal chocolates from my drawer,

I will write songs about you,

and when, we will make it to the end,

we will stay forever in the graveyard.

20. I Love Every Version Of You!

I tell you how much I love you all the time,

but I never really explain why I feel that way,

so I'm going to do that now.

I love the way your voice sounds when you say my name.

I love the way your smile tilts when trying not to laugh.

I love the way your kisses magnetically feel against my neck.

I love the way your voice sounds, even if you hate it.

I love the girl you were when I met you and

I love the girl I can see you growing into.

I love every version of you.

I love every messy piece of yours.

21. You Are My Soul

You're the person I can tell my secrets to,

the first person I want to talk to when I wake up,

and last person I want to talk to before I drift off to sleep.

When something good happens,

you're the first person I want to tell.

When I'm troubled by something or if I get a bad news,

you're the one I go to for support.

But you're so much more to me than a friend

or someone who helps me in tough times,

you're the love of my life.

You're my friend, my lover, my comfort, and my strength.

I am so lucky to have you...

Six

1. Yes I Cry

I cry. Not because I want to gain

sympathy from you but I feel comfortable

enough to share my true feelings with you.

I know you won't make fun of me, instead

you'll make me understand that crying isn't

the solution, standing up whenever I fall is.

I cry in front of you because know you are

there to wipe my tears, to hug me tight and

to calm me down. I know I can trust you to

share every little thing with you, to put my

life completely naked in front of you.

I cry because I know you won't take advantage

of my vulnerability, instead you will give me

every ounce of love and advice to make me

feel that I am never alone as you are always

there with me to guide me and give me

all the support I need.

2. Yes, I Am A Complicated Person

I don't like to express anything but I remember everything.

I like to notice things & this is

both a beautiful and terrible thing because

I will always remember the way you smile

since I've watched it countless times.

I know little details about you that you've forgotten

you have told me because my mind doesn't

let me forget them. It's who I am.

On the flip side there's still me through all

of it - a person I think can't possibly be

as interesting as you. I am full of thoughts

and feelings that I don't know how to say out

loud sometimes.

So, yes, I am a hard person to love because

I look at you in one way but myself in another.

3. Have You?

Have you ever looked into someone's eyes for so long

that it felt like a sin to look away?

Have you ever held anyone else's hand so tightly

That your fingers felt empty and void after letting go?

Have you ever kissed someone so passionately and delirously

That the taste of their lips remained imprinted on yours?

Have you ever had anyone whisper sweet nothings to you

While you could feel their breaths tingling close to your ears

The words of which resonated in your heart for days?

Have you ever penetrated into someone's soul so deeply

That you could see the demons lurking beneath?

Have you ever loved so ardently that

That one emotion stayed permanently rooted to your heart?

Have you ever given up every last ounce you had to give

Only to receive nothing in return?

Have you all ever healed another heart

Only to get yours broken?

4. One For Self Love

Stand in front of the mirror at the end of

the day and question yourself, "did you smile today?"

And if the answer is "no",

then make efforts to wear a beautiful smile every day.

Just because that beautiful and

bright smile will heal every pain of yours.

Don't let your smile be killed by someone

who doesn't care about it.

Be your self hero,

Be your self partner,

Be your self motivator,

Be the reason behind your smile.

Let your smile kill their ego,

Let your smile kill their ignorance,

Let your smile melt their hearts,

Let your smile kill your pain and

Let your smile be your stressbuster.

5. Be Together

It's only when we are together,

my smile becomes the widest ,

my heart beats the fastest and

I feel the luckiest person alive,

the moon spread its charm and

shines the brighest ever, the stars

cover up the whole sky with their

little cute twinkles, the breeze tends

to touch us with colder hands than

before, the world happens to stop

at our sight silent and serene,

and I feel like gifting you the entire

Universe of all the happy things that

You have missed till now..

6. From Girl's Side

All of a sudden,

I miss warmth in your friendship.

I no longer miss your texts and calls.

I have turned my self into a

cold hearted person not to miss you anymore.

You don't appreciate my presence now

when I care for you,

when I love for and

when I am there you all the times.

You have started you

taking me for granted.

Deep down,

I still hope you will miss

my absence someday.

I'm sure you will never crave for my presence, still,

I am loving you the same now as then..

7. *It's Because Of YOU.*

I don't have an answer for that, but I guess it's just the vibes you give me, face, the laughs I get from talking to you, and just the fact that you the smiles you put on my can make me think of you even if we aren't talking at that moment. I honestly cannot say there's an answer to that, but I will say that you are the reason I am happy each and every day.

8. *Love Is All About Caring*

You know you are in love when you can

say anything to the person and you know

they won't laugh at you. When you can

see their face when you close your eyes.

When you can still taste their kiss after you

have said goodbye. You can tell you're in

love when you miss them before they are

gone. When their voice lingers in your ears.

When their presence eases your pain. When

they are the only thing you can think about.

When they call you at 4 in the morning to

"I Love You" and mean it. When say,

tears stain their heart also. When they are

hurt just because of these tears. Ultimately,

you know you are in love when you can't

imagine living without them....

9. One Day

And one day she realized she no longer

had to hold onto the feelings that hurt

her heart. She can simply allow herself

to feel them and then when she is ready

she can gently let them go and

set herself free.

10. It's Okay

It's okay to be afraid. It's okay if you don't know yet who you are. We all have different timelines of discovering life, our own unique ways of figuring things out. May be you still don't know if the path you are taking is right for you. It's okay, don't judge yourself for not knowing everything. We all find our ways through falling and rising, by taking chances. There is no shortcut to live this life, and if we keep on waiting for the right time or the right way to truly start living it, we will be waiting here forever.

11. I Feel Found By You

I feel found by your eyes, where other eyes wouldn't dare to see.

Found by your hands when you slowly and softly touch my palm with your thumb. When you mess with my hair. When you poke my nose.

Found by your laugh, when I say something I didn't mean to, because I'm not used to being heard.

Found by your heartbeat, pressed against mine when you hold me close.

Found by your smell, smeared in all my clothes.

Found by your texts. By your calls. By your pictures.

Every piece of me feels found by you. Every bit of my soul has been seen like it hasn't been seen before. As if you were the only one that saw me in a sea of lost faces.

And sometimes it feels weird, being so self-conscious. Because everything about you makes me think about everything about me. But in a good way. Because the song is right. I'ma flightless bird that fell in love with a never landing king of the sky. So let me ask you, please, Now that you found me, don't let me go.

12. It's All About YOU

The sparkle in your eye,

The warmth of your skin.

Your breath on my neck,

That quivers within.

The touch of your hand,

The smell of your hair.

The kindness in your smile,

That strength in your stare.

Your kiss on my lips,

Your body near mine.

The stroke of your touch,

That feeling inside.

The sound of your voice,

Compassion in your embrace.

The serenity in your stride,

The power in your face.

The calming of your presence,

The beating of your heart.

The promise of tomorrow,

That we may never part.

The beauty of your kiss,

and that magic in your touch.

It is for all these reasons and more,

Why I love you so much.

13. I'll Be Always There For You

When you are sad, I will dry your tears

When you are scared, I will comfort your fears

When you need love, my heart I will share

When you are sick, for you I will care

You will feel my love when we are apart

Knowing that nothing will change my heart

When you are worried, I will give you hope

When you are confused, I will help you cope

When you are lost, and can't see the light

My love will be a beacon, shining ever so bright.

14. She Loves You.

You may not be her first, her last, or her only. She loved before she may love again. But if she loves you now, what else matters? She's not perfect-you aren't either, and the two of you may never be perfect together but if she can make you laugh, cause you to think twice, and admit to being human and making mistakes, hold onto her and give her the most you can. She may not be thinking about you every second of the day, but she will give you a part of her that she knows you can break-her heart. So don't hurt her, don't change her, don't analyze and don't expect more than she can give. Smile when she makes you happy, let her know when she makes you mad, and miss her when she's not there.

15. Realisation Of LOVE

You came into my life unexpectedly,

and everything took a turn for the better.

Your warm eyes, your laugh,

the sincere way you speak,

and the kindness you showed me,

all became a part of my life.

As you unfolded yourself to me,

I discovered more and more beauty.

I have never seen so much

gentleness in one person.

Without even knowing it,

you were slowly making a place

for yourself in my heart.

It used to seem so hard at times

to feel so close in a relationship.

But it's so easy to feel close to you.

I can't tell you how nice that feels.

I realize now that I had never known

what it meant to be loved

until I was loved by you.

16. You Are Mine

Where are you tonight my love?

What is it that you do?

It's true my heart is torn apart

When I'm not with you

What enchanted thoughts swim through your head?

Are any of them of me?

When, my dear, you go to bed

Is it my face you see?

Who is honoured with your presence now?

And do they even care?

The thought of you not being admired

Fills me with despair

Do they appreciate your loveliness?

Do they marvel at your splendor?

Do they love to hear your velvet voice?

Do they adore your smile so tender?

If they do not

Then they all are fools

and had you been with me

Every day, my love, you'd be a queen

because that's what you are to me

I'm at your feet

and I come with gifts

my body, heart, and soul

They're yours to do with as you please

to command and to control

I give myself with all my heart

I'm yours for all of time

Your king, your anything

only say that you are mine..

17. Love Doesn't Ask, Love Only Says

Love doesn't ask

"Who are you...!"

Love only says

"You are mine.!"

Love doesn't ask

"Where are you from..!"

Love only says

"You live in my heart.!"

Love doesn't ask

"What do you do...!"

Love only says

"You make my heart to beat..!"

Love doesn't ask

"Why are you far away !!"

Love only says

"You are always with me far away!"

18. You Are A Diamond In The Coal Mine

Your lips, your eyes, your soul

Are like a work of art,

The most creative thing of all

Is your beautiful heart.

If you were a painting,

No colours could express

The beauty deep inside you,

A rainbow, nothing less.

If you were a sculpture

The clay could hardly make

Your figure of an angel

Without one mistake.

If you were a euphony

No choir could really sing

All the beautiful music

Your eyes could possibly bring.

So here I am, an artist,

With inspiration beyond belief

But to capture such rare beauty,

I'd have to be a thief...

19. End Like This

How do I start?

What do I say?

I love you and you take my breath away?

Do I say hold me tight, keep me warm all through the night?

So how do I start?

I start like this: hold me, love me, teach me, move me, motivate me to do something great.

Now that I've started, how do I end?

I end like this

I LOVE YOU!

20. What I want?

I want to find you in all the poems I read,

I want to wake up and smell the earth that smells like you,

I want to listen to you in every bird that sings,

I want to hear your breath everytime the ocean breaks at my feet,

I want to feel your touch every time a blossom falls on me, and

I want to hold your hand everytime I see something beautiful, because there is no beauty, if it isn't with you.

21. Worthy

I wish that I could make her realize that she's worthy of being loved. That she could be someone's world. That somebody thinks of her every single night before she goes to bed and every single morning when she wakes up. That someone nearly dies with yearning thinking of her arms around him. That somebody loves her more than anything because she's fantastic.

Seven

1. It's Late

It's late.. I just wanna come lay with you.. I wanna listen to you breathe.. and kiss your face softly and run my fingers through your hair. i want to feel your hand on my leg pulling me closer.. I want that deep eye contact.. you have the most beautiful eyes.. that grin. looking away because you're smiling too big only to have me turn your chin and kiss you more.. I want the laughter, and the vulnerable moments.. it's late.. and I MISS YOU.

2. Let's Run Away

Let's run away together, away from the city lights, where no one knows our names yet. And we can see the stars at night, we'll camp out in the open, warming cold skin by the fire, tell each other hopes and dreams, and all of our desires. We'll own nothing more than we need, watch sunrises colour the sky. Learn what we're really here for, away from society's eyes, this journey will be scary, but we'll leave without a plan. And I know it will be alright, as long as you're holding my hand.

3. Need To Be Loved

I love you.

Not the concept of you.

Not the perception of you.

Not what you will become.

Not your prospects.

Not your need to be loved. I love you. Today. Right now. Just as you are.
And I know, with time we will change. We will evolve. We will grow. And I
hope we do all of it together. But I don't ask anything from you other than
what we have now. I don't expect you to promise me anything in return.
Because I love you for you, and the promises you are unable to make today
don't change anything.

4. Immortal Love

There couldn't be a thing in this world that could replace you. Honestly you
are the person from my dreams. I couldn't ask for something other than the
angel that you are. How much can I possibly love you? I could ask myself
that a thousand times and I wouldn't land you a real answer. The truth is
that every other day that answer changes, because I love you even more as
each day passes. That may be the only rational answer to that difficult

question. I just couldn't bear to imagine myself without you as my confidant. My love for you is the only thing in this plain world that I cannot express myself of how I feel. My love for you confuses me. My love for you is immortal.

5. It's Not To Easy To Fall In Love

I wasn't looking for anything at all when I met you. Actually, I wasn't planning on falling for anyone so soon. But then I met you. And that was it.. I guess things just happened. I found you and I found myself slowly wanting to spend time with you. It was simple. It was easy. And I think that's how the best relationships begin. You're not looking for anything and then suddenly you realize; you have something..

6. I Can't Wait For You To Love

I can't wait to wake up to morning kisses, hugs from behind only a few hours after seeing each other. I'm so excited to roll over in my sleep and to crash into you with my arms and legs pulling you in. I can't wait to drink coffee together only moments before having to leave with kisses pressed to smiles to go to work, knowing I'll see you when I come home. I'm looking forward to sitting in the kitchen floor eating bad take out food, laughing over glasses of wine and the things that felt so stressful during the day. I can't wait to banter over you sneaking to read my writing before I've shown you. I'm so excited to look at the tickle fights, the touches that aren't sexual but just slight touches of comfort. I can't wait to stay up watching tv shows and movies, and getting obsessed over small things together. I can't wait to take pictures of you in your purest forms, to hang around the house. I can't wait to get a puppy together, to make plans together, to travel together and to simply love together. I am so damn excited to find you and to learn all about you, and to love the things about yourself that are hard to love just as much as the things about you that are so easy to love. I am so excited for you, but I'm even more excited for me. It's going to be such an honor to love you. *I can't wait for you to love me.*

7. Non-Existent Love

Bursting in laughter

A never ending touch running through my veins

Kisses on the cheek

Caresses on my lips, you brushed yours against mine

With a vivid background music

It is not meaningless; our kiss...

It is as sensual as soft tickling on my neck

As passionate as the storm,

A storm purifies the atmosphere

A passion purifies the soul

But my love for you is non-existent.

8. Atmosphere

When I look at you I see waves caressing the shore and sunlight sneaking through the trees. I hear your voice and it's like birds singing in the morning and the laughter of old friends. Being held in your arms feels like the warmth of a gentle bonfire and the subtle summer breeze. When I'm with you I experience a whole new world.

9. Broken Person

When you love a broken person everything about them will be fragile so don't let go when they curl into a tiny ball.

Everytime someone hurts them because these broken people will be seen as sensitive and every little thing will irritate their small heart but,

I promise you that the love of a broken person is just something no star can put together

They will make you a shelter in their broken heart, only so your happiness is protected

And they will also laugh along with your word that hurt them

Broken people will love you from their heart, even when every part of theirs you ruin

Because with broken people even if their hearts were made of dirt

They'll eventually turn into the purest people walking on Earth.

10. Don't Hurry For Love

To be in a relationship means that you care about your partner. It sounds easy but in reality it takes time and effort. If you decide to be in relation with a person it has to be out of love. And you have to be clear what this actually means. It is not only good times, sex and someone who you can always chill with. You have to understand that after this point her problems are yours. Her pain is your pain.

11. Trustworthy Person

Be with someone who you don't have to hide from, in any way. Whether it's your morning face before you've put your make up on, an embarrassing story to tell about something that happened on your way home, or an ambition you've had since you were six. make sure you end up with someone who knows all of it and still loves you. A person you can tell your whole life to is a person worth spending a life with.

12. She Really Deserves Infinite Love

Her heartbeat dropped into 40 per minute, her pupil grew so much I could read her mind. Her deep brown eyes looked so lovely at me that I swore to me I could never hurt her, even if she deserves it, I don't want to see these eyes crying. I felt her heart beating and her voice whispering "I am so happy to have you" and then she just fell asleep on my chest. A tear flowed down my cheek, because I knew she is the one.

13. Addicted To Your Love

I don't know how to explain it anymore. Your company is indescribable for me, I feel so fulfilled, as I would be weightless, like on the best drug on earth. I feel like that this is my destiny, to be with you forever and not more nor less. I feel like my obligation is to make you happy whatever it is I want to see you smile. And that is what I should feel like, because what we have is love, real love.

14. Love Can Take On Many Different Forms

Love can be waking up in the morning, looking in the mirror, and smiling because the sun is shining and your eyes are sparkling. Love can be the glimpse you give your boy or girlfriend, than one split second where you know that their feelings for you are real. love can be your friend giving you chocolate because you're nervous for an exam to come. love can be hugging your mother or brother or grandma or whoever you feel like hugging. love is taking a bath and falling asleep to music because you can't get enough. love is thunder and storm and rain and dirty shoes and scraped knees. love is studying and giving your best. love is everywhere; love for who you are; love for who you want to become; love for what you're doing; love for those around you. without love the world would be hopeless. so thank god that it's here all the time. we just have to realise that it is.

15. I Will Be Here

If in the morning when you wake,

If the sun does not appear,

I will be here.

If in the dark we lose sight of love,

Hold my hand and have no fear,

I will be here.

I will be here,

When you feel like being quiet,

When you need to speak your mind I will listen.

Through the winning, losing, and trying we'll be together,

And I will be here.

If in the morning when you wake,

If the future is unclear,

I will be here.

As sure as seasons were made for change,

Our lifetimes were made for years,

I will be here.

16. I Will Love You There

If I could make it better, I would. I would swallow the sun and kiss it straight into your mouth if it meant you'd feel warm again. I would bury green gardens deep inside your heart if it meant you would blossom there. I would pull myself apart, jagged bone and soft skin, if it meant I could find the right pieces to put you back together again. I would, darling. I would. But can't. For I learned time and time again that human beings cannot be saved, or fixed, or grown by - they can only be loved. So I will love you, and I will love you well. I will love you on the days your laughter meets your eyes, and will love you just as much when it does not. I will love you on the days you are made of light, and I will love you just as much when the world feels like a load you have to carry upon your shoulders. I will love you through your healing, and I will love you through your hurt. I will love you through your peace, and I will love you through your pain. I will love you when you love yourself, and I will love you when you do not. I refuse to fall in love with the idea of who you can be if I were to nip and tuck and patch and sew you into someone else. If I were to throw a blanket over the baggage in your ribcage, only focusing on the prettiest parts of you. I refuse to love you in halves. So – show me where you thrive, and I will love you there. Show me where you break and I will love you there. Show me where you hope and I will love you there. Show me where you doubt and I will love you there. Show me where you hide, and I will love you there. Show me your open heart, flayed and beating in its decay and in its growth, and I will love it, darling. I will love it.

17. Kiss Her

Kiss her. Slowly, take your time, there's no place you'd rather be. Kiss her but not like you're waiting for something else, like your hands beneath her shirt or her skirt or tangled up in her bra straps. Nothing like that. Kiss her like you've forgotten any other mouth that your mouth has ever touched. Kiss her with a curious childish delight. Laugh into her mouth, inhale her sighs. Kiss her until she moans. Kiss her with her face in your hands. Or your hands in her hair. Or pulling her closer at the waist. Kiss her like you want to take her dancing. Like you want to spin her into an open arena and watch her look at you like you're the brightest thing she's ever seen. Kiss her like she's the brightest thing you've ever seen. Take your time. Kiss her like the first and only piece of chocolate you're ever going to taste. Kiss her until she forgets how to count. Kiss her stupid. Kiss her silent.

18. My Day Starts With Her

When I wake up every morning

I always watch you for a while

Then I kiss you very lightly,

Watch you lips turn to a smile.

Then you ask me what the time is

And I whisper in your ear

That the hour hardly matters

When you're lying warm and near.

Your smile grows slightly wider,

But you turn your face away,

Hide your head under the pillow,

Try to cheat the break of day.

Your hair wisps round about you,

Flows like water to your hips,

But your neck soon bare before me

Feels the pressure of my lips.

Then I touch you very lightly,

Run my fingers down your spine,

And your body gently waking

Turns till eyes gaze into mine.

And in that very moment,

As your mouth seeks to entice,

When I wake up every morning,

I am lost in paradise.

19. You Make My Nights Beautiful

I lie on the ground,

and stare into space,

the stars start to move,

into the shape of your face.

I see you there now,

looking down at me,

with that cute little smile,

that I like to see.

You say "close your eyes",

"tell me what you see",

I see only two people,

just you and me.

We're walking the shoreline,

with our feet getting wet,

the horizon turns pink,

as the sun starts to set.

We make love through the night,

on that white sandy shore,

then I hold you while thinking,

I could want nothing more.

OhI wish I could be,

in that one special place,

as I lie on the ground,

and I stare into space...

20. You Are That Someone

I honestly just need someone to come into my life that really genuinely cares about me and wants to sit and have long conversations about things that actually matter and wants to go on adventures late at night and wants to be there for me at my lowest points and celebrate with me at my highest points and just be the rock that keeps me going when life gets rough.

21. Baby Girl

The sun has finally arrived. As the warmer weather rolls in, I cannot help but think about al the fun we are going to have together under this roaring summer sun. I spend my mornings thinking about waking up with you, walking in the morning glow, holding hands and laughing on our way to grab an early coffee. I spend my daytimes dreaming about exploring new cities, climbing new mountains, forging new paths and building our dreams together. I spend the evenings hoping for your skin on my skin, our lips together - with late-night words, or late-night kisses, but also thinking of evenings out and vibrant city parties and sneaking into exciting events together. I am looking forward to a life with you, a life without limits. As you build your character there, I am building a life for us here - something exciting, and passionate, and meaningful. I can't wait to share it with you.

Eight

1. Future In Her Eyes

Because when I look into your eyes, I don't see just a starry sky, I see a whole galaxy built just for me to explore. I could find whole new constellations that no one would ever find out about because its my galaxy. I love you because when I'm with you I feel safer than I've ever felt in my whole life. People always say you know you're home when you feel safe, but sometimes its not where your home is, its with whom. I love you because I can see us together 10 years from now. I can't see where or doing what, but I know I want to spend a long, long time with you.

2. I Love YOU Infinity

I can give you thousands of reasons for loving you. But that wouldn't be true. That will be mere justification of loving you after I fell in love with you. Not the real reason. Hopefully, rest of my life will be good enough to find the answer of this question. If not, then maybe in the 6 more afterlives. If I still fail miserably then, please forgive me, can't stop loving you.

3. She Is WORTHY To Be Loved

You must learn her.

You must know the reason why she is silent.

You must trace her weakest spots.

You must write to her.

You must remind her that you are there.

You must know how long it takes for her to give up.

You must be there to hold her when she is about to.

You must love her because many have tried and failed,

She wants to know that she is worthy to be loved, that she is worthy to be kept.

And, this is how you keep her.

4. I Promise That I Will Never You

I am giving you this ring as a promise to you

That no matter what, I will always be here and I will always be true

I promise that I will lie with you and hold you at night

When things throughout your day just don't seem to be going right

For you, I would walk a thousand miles and more

Just to see your beautiful smile that I absolutely adore

I promise that I will make you smile when you feel like crying

I promise that I will comfort you if you feel like dying

I promise to steal away your every sorrow and fear

I promise to wipe away your every tear

I promise to cherish every minute I spend with you

Until the daylight sky is no longer the color of blue

Without your love, I do not know what I would do

I will not have a future unless it involves you

You've changed me for the better and I have never been so happy

Now, with you in my life, I can't picture a world without you and me

Fate decided it was time for us to be together

And though our time here on Earth is short,

I promise I want you always and forever

I promise that no matter what may happen we will make it through

Please take this ring as a symbol of the love I will always have for you.!

5. She Cares For ME

They say that love is like wind; you can't see it, but you can feel it. But baby, with you, I see it. It's in your deep brown eyes that light up with your shy smile. It's the timid way you giggle. It's the way you wake up in the middle of the night just to hold my hand. It's the way you hold me when I'm scared. It's the way you talk to me a little bit longer even though you know you'll be tired in the morning. It's the way you make sure I get home safely. It's the way you gently pull me into a kiss when we haven't seen each other in a couple of days. It's so much more than a feeling.

6. I Love Her Deep Brown EYES

I love the way her eyes spark when we're talking or when she's telling me something she wants me to know, the way she mouths the words to herself when she's reading and concentrating, the way she looks at me as if there's only me, as if she can see past the flesh and bone and bullshit right into me that's there, the one I don't even see myself.

7. Judging Is Toxic

I love you means that I accept you for the person that you are, and that I do not wish to change you into someone else. It means that I will love you and stand by you even through the worst of times. It means loving you even when you're down, not just when you're fun to be around. 'I Love You' means that I know your deepest darkest secrets and yet not judge you for them, asking in return that you do not judge me for mine. It means that I care enough to fight for what we have and that I love you enough to let go. It means thinking of you, dreaming of you, wanting and needing you constantly, and hoping that you feel the same way for me.

8. You Are All I Need

You're the thought that starts each morning,

The conclusion to each day.

You are in all that I do,

And everything I say.

You're the smile on my face,

The twinkle in my eye.

The warmth inside my heart,

The fullness in my life.

You're the hand that's laced in mine,

And the coat upon my back.

My friend, my love,

My shoulder to lean on.

You're my silly, mature, caring,

Thoughtful, bright, and honest girl.

The one who holds me tightly,

When I need the world.

You're the dimple in my cheek,

The ever-constant tingle in my soul.

The voice that makes me weak,

The happiness of my life.

You are all I've wanted,

You are all I need.

You are all I've dreamed of,

You are all of this to me.

9. Connection Of Souls

I will spend my entire life trying to give you all the love that you deserve.
You are the missing piece to the puzzle of my heart. I have been feeling
extremely lonely this week and I just wanted to tell you that I appreciate
you on such a deep level that I feel as if any distance, and any time period,
is surmontable because of how perfectly your soul fits within the embrace of
mine.

10. *Why I Am In Love With You*

You wanna know "Why I'm in love with you?" she asked as she ran her hand along my jaw. "Sure," I answered feeling as if my heart could explode at any moment." I fell in love with the way your laugh is always the loudest in the forest or the way your facial expressions always give away how you feel. The way you smile & freak out when you see puppies makes my heart want you. Or when you take a shower & your hair starts to curl & when you say you hate it I don't understand because to me it's fucking beautiful. I fell in love with the way you feel so intensely & your sarcasm is something that I just can't live without. & the way you want everyone to be happy gives me hope that not everyone in the world is cruel. I love how sunsets and thunderstorm bring you pure joy. And you have the faith of a child that makes me want to protect you even though you're the strongest person I know. I'm in love with everything that has to do with you.

11. *Sunday's*

And most of all, I want to do nothing with you. I want to spend a Sunday at home, me in my corner, you in yours, reading or working or writing, silently in our spaces. I want to be so together that we don't have to say anything at all, that we can just watch it rain and drink our tea and occasionally look at one another and smile. I will wonder why I ever

thought that Sunday was for running errands and cleaning and getting
things done one after the other, when it is so clear that spending them
silently across from you is so much better. I want to have every bit of
Sunday with you, every Sunday, because you are simply too good to end on
a Saturday night.

12. Maybe

Maybe you don't end up with the person your heart chooses. Maybe that's
not how life works. Maybe you don't get what you want. Maybe you end up
finding what you need, and maybe the Universe knows what you need more
than you do. Maybe love changes. Maybe it goes from "I'll wait up and call
you after work," to "I'm going to sleep, I'm tired." Maybe it goes from "You
have nothing to worry about," to "I really wish you didn't overthink so
much." Maybe it goes from "I choose you," to "I have to choose myself
right now." Maybe love isn't one of those things that grows with certain
people. Maybe you become too big for it. Maybe it becomes too
uncomfortable, too small for who you change into. Maybe it's like that
sweater you always loved growing up, or your childhood bed. You learn to
appreciate it for what it was, but you come to terms with the fact that you
have outgrown it. You learn to let it go. And maybe letting go of love isn't
some loud celebration at the end of a dark tunnel. Maybe letting go is the
moment you decide that you can no longer keep the past alive inside of

you. Maybe it is quiet, maybe there is no checklist, or way of telling if it has actually happened. Maybe it is simply just you learning how to release your grip, how to let things be, how to lay down your arms. Maybe that is how it's done – in the silence of it all, in the calmness of everyday life. I am starting to learn that maybe walking away is the best thing you can do for yourself, and for the person you love. Maybe walking away is you making peace with the fact that sometimes things and people and happiness changes. Maybe it is the bravest thing you can do. Maybe, when you walk away, you're not making the biggest mistake of your life. Maybe, when you walk away, your life is just beginning..

13. Face Whatever Comes In Between

Real love has little to do with falling. It's a climb up the rocky face of a mountain, hard work, and most people are too selfish or too scared to bother. Very few reach the critical point in their relationship that summons the attention of the light and the dark, that place where they will make a commitment to love no matter what obstacles-or temptations- appear in their path.

14. Middle Of The Night

It's the middle of the night and I'm thinking about you, not in any particular way, just of you. I wonder if you're up too or if you're sleeping what it is you're dreaming about? I wonder if you were here, would you pull me close or just stay a safe distance? Would you give in to your heart's desires as you lay here half asleep, your eyes barely open and your raspy voice that I'm sure would sound delightful to my ears, would you cave in for just a moment? Just long enough for me to feel you against my skin and have this moment ease it's way, way into my heart. It's the middle of the night and if you were here that would be the only thing that would make this better.

15. You're So Impossible To Describe

You make me forget about all the bad thing with just one glance. Your arms are so strong and they hold me so tight and it's these moments: Held in your embrace My head on your chest, feeling your heart beating My fingers intertwined in yours. It's these moments when I find myself falling for you. I know I've tried to stay away from falling again, but inwardly I cannot help but feel like there's no other way to describe this feeling. Because there is no better place to be than with you. Your hands fit perfectly into the spaces between my fingers and these memories are what keep me awake through the day. Your fingers tracing circles on my skin. Our legs; an entanglement of limbs.

16. Misunderstandings

In a world that seeks connection we oddly avoid eye contact, we time our text responses in order to protect ourselves from seeming too eager or too interested, and we hold our feelings back because we don't want to seem overly emotional or unreasonable. We silence our instincts, and at the end of the day instead of feeling good about ourselves, we feel alone, we feel misunderstood. Remember - it is okay to be emotional, to seek help, to confidently tell someone you enjoy being around that you are infatuated with them. There is nothing wrong with vulnerability, with being human, for that is what creates depth within our relationships, and that is what ultimately unifies us.

17. Beyond Expectations

You and I are connected in a way that goes beyond romance, beyond friendship, beyond what we've ever had before. It has defied time, distance, and changes in ourselves and in our lives. It has defied every explanation. Except one: Pure and simply, we're soul mates. I can't explain, I just feel it. It's there in the way my spirits lift whenever we talk. The sound of your voice brings me home, in a way I can't explain. It's in the delight I feel, when we laugh at exactly the same things. When I'm with you, it's like a tiny piece of the universe shifts into place. A place it's supposed to be, and all is right with the world. These things and so many more, have made me understand that this is a once in a lifetime, forever connection. A connection that could only exist between you and me. And deep in my soul, I know that our relationship is a rare gift. One that brings us extraordinary happiness all through our lives.

18. If You Let Me LOVE You

If you let me love you.. I would love how the sun leaves lipstick stains on your skin. I would love the way you drink your morning coffee. I would love the way I can trace constellations in the spaces between your teeth when you smile. I would love the hue of your eyes and freckles splashed across your nose and face. I would love the way you drink your morning milk & take bites of thin egg. I would love the way you get excited because of an unexpected movie ending. I would love the way you miss your childhood friend and the thin pancakes your mom was making each Sunday. I would love the way you explore new places and take notes. If you let me love you, I would love you the way nature intended you to be loved..

19. I Wish I Were..

I wish I were a bird

every morning I would fly to your place

and sit at the window

to be the first one everyday

to see your lovely face

I wish I were the dew

when you pick the rose

and smell its scent

I would silently wish you morning

and kiss you on your nose

I wish I were the mirror

the mirror on your wall

when you would ask me

I would tell you my love

you are the fairest of them all

Every morning when you pray

I wish I were the sun rays

to see you and be your admirer

and pray for your happiness

God bless you with grace

Oh if, I were... I wish I were

or be me only

singing to you the song of love

if you would hear only.

Singing to you till my death.

20. LET ME...

Let me take care of your broken heart

and show you how to fly.

Let me hold you gently by the hand

and kiss your tears goodbye.

Let me lead you to tomorrow's light

and out of needless rain,

'cause all I want right now

is to see you smile again.

Let me sing you all the songs I wrote

'til you sleep in my embrace,

and I'll keep you safe and warm until

the sunlight strokes your face.

Let me bring you up the mountain's peak,

and I'll let you touch the skies

to remind you of the strength I see

when I look into your eyes.

Let me kiss and show you what is love

and the happiness it brings.

You'll sail again like a butterfly

endowed with pretty wings.

Let me do all these to let you see

our fates are intertwined.

You're the accidental precious gem

I've waited long to find.

The earth and sky conspired to make us meet.

They knew we both belong

to each other like words and lovely notes

give life to every song.

So fly with me, my beautiful one.

It's time we leave the past.

I'm yours to keep, and you are mine.

We're finally home at last.

21. It's You

If there's one face I want to see,

so beautiful, so true,

one smile that makes a difference,

to everything I do.

If there's one touch I long to feel,

one voice I long to hear,

whenever I am happy,

or just needing someone near.

If there's one joy, one love,

from which I never want to part,

it's you, my very special love,

my world, my life, my heart.

Nine

1. I'mmature

I want someone that's going to be a massive weirdo with me and stays up really late getting wasted and having profound conversations and going for long drives without destination and will sing duets with me and react funny scenes from cool movies and musicals but I also want them to be able to calm the fuck down and shut up and not feel like they need to fill the silence with pointless banter and just cuddle till we fall asleep.

2. I'd Die for YOU

Candles flicker softly on a table set for two,

There's no one on the earth tonight except for me and you.

A nice romantic dinner and a bottle of chilled wine,

And we are here together in a moment stopped in time.

A love so few have ever known and this is its birth night,

Alone within our little world, you and I and candlelight.

So soon we will set free the feelings that we want to share.

And I am held here spellbound by your laughter in the air. Thoughts of love
like falling leaves,

Swirling in the autumn breeze,

Flow in our minds and in our eyes,

A tender look and longing sighs,

We touch and as the fire starts,

That we have kindled in our hearts,

We kiss and hear the angels sing,

As heavens gift to me you bring,

No more to live my life alone,

And in your soul I found my home,

At peace within your loving arms,

Captivated by your charms,

And happily I'd die for you,

3. What I Want!

I want you. I want your sleepy confused look when you wake up. I want to
be the warmth that fills the space in your bed. I want to be the sheets your
fingers crave at night; the blanket that wraps around you all night. I want to
drink tea with you, share some records we find. I want to talk about
everything in the world newspapers. I want to discuss with you, to be
stubborn and quick-witted with you. I want to have differences between us.
I want your flaws. All of them. I want go into the deepest corners of your
mind and never get bored of you. I want to be surprised by the new all the
time. I want to look at you like a movie, a living piece of art; always trying
to chase what you crave. and capture you.

4. Let Me Share Your Pain

I look at you

and I can see it in your face

you think you hide it,

but I see you.

I see the hurt

the dark circles beneath your eyes

and the quiet plea

dancing on your bottom lip,

too afraid to be voiced

too afraid to be heard

because you're too afraid

to be hurt

and I just want to take you and

wrap you up in my arms

hold you, console you

tell you things that you'll believe

but you don't seem to believe

anything anymare

because you have been deceived

far too many times

so I'll just look at you

and see the pain in your fake smile, and I'll smile back

and I'll hear the attempted deception when you tell me that

you're just tired,

and I'll say me too

I know you're broken inside,

I can see it in your face

violets are blue,

and so are you.

5. *Real Romance*

I think a lot of people don't understand what real romance is. Anyone can buy flowers, candy and jewelry, there's no love in that. The truly romantic things in life are those little things you do every day to show you care, and that you are thinking of them. It's going out of our way to make them happy. The way you hold her hand when you know she's scared, or you save the last piece of cake for him. The random texts in the middle of the day, just to say "I love you" or "I miss you". The way he stops to kiss you when he passes by. It's dedicating your favorite song to her, and letting her eat your fries; telling her she's beautiful , even she's in her sweats; with her hair in a ponytail and no makeup. It's putting your favorite show on pause so she can tell you about her day, and laughing at his jokes, even the really lame ones. It's slow dancing in the kitchen and kissing in the rain. Romance isn't about buying, it's about giving. True romance is in gestures.

6. *There Is No HATE Between US*

We sit hand in hand and our fingers interlace, I sit and I stare, trying to figure you out, exploring the beauty of your face, wondering what is it that we're getting ourselves into. when our fingers first interlaced I saw your face light up, and saw how fast a smile appeared on your face, I heard the sound of happiness coming from your mounth, I heard the sound of the little chirp you made, and I felt you holding my hand tighter. I felt the urge to see you, I couldn't wait no more, I saw you and I felt the rush, the rush of excitement, the rush of happiness and love, I was afraid to run so I trotted, I trotted towards you and gave you a hug. I felt you, I didn't want to let go, such a tight hug, best one I've ever had, I looked up and we both went in, there'd it go, a kiss, we smiled in between and even laughed too, I felt happy, there was happiness all around and love too and nothing else, I felt as if that day would never come, all I wanted was you, it was just you in that moment, it was just us, us in the moment, that was all that mattered to me.

7. I Love Your Voice

I never loved the sound of my name so much until I saw it bloom on your tongue. Until I felt it pressed against my skin, sweet, pure and hot. I love the way you say it in the morning, our bodies folding into each other like delicate paper cranes. I love the way you say it over coffee, the warmth of your voice to tend to all my heartaches. I love the way you say it over the phone. Soft, like a sigh. Carrying me the distance from my bed to yours. I love the way you say it in the twilight. Enchanting me like a prayer, my knees dropped to the floor. I never loved the sound of my name so much until I saw the way it tasted in your mouth. Like the sweetest peach, you savor it slow. The purest taste of budding love.

8. From a Broken Girl to The Boy

All you left behind were scars. all you left behind was fury. all you left behind was pain. again and again 'cause you're leaving so often. but it's not your fault. it's mine. i'm making the mistake again and again. i'm taking you back everytime. i'm forgiving you every single fucking time although you don't deserve it anymore. you're just making it harder and harder for me and

it's like,everytime i'm trying to stand up you push me down again. it's not
even your purpose but it's still hard. you were my everything lately and
now.. after one month of space, all i can remember is what you did to me.
our memories are still there and how i felt about you too but i'm not able to
remember because i'm pushing it away so hard. i don't want to remember. i
don't want it to be like in our memories again. i don't want this anymore. i
need to push you away and stop taking you back. i finally realized,i need to
end some things in my life before they end me.. and sorry, but you're one of
them.

9. Act Of Love

It's crazy. Due all the time I spend working on my inner peace and
calmness, while I'm trying to be the person always staying cool and being
someone who doesn't know violence, I never found a weakness. there was
nothing that has ever driven me as crazy as it drives me when it's about you.
my nerves just can't stand the pressure I feel when I get the feeling that I
need to worry. I'm so sensitive when it come's to you and I would do
anything to protect and help you if I had to. and I mean it. I would give up
all the work I did and I would lose myself for a while if it's necessary. I can't
even control it. no matter how hard I'm trying to stay calm and not worry
or keep a positive attitude, my mind turns off when it comes to you. you're
my biggest weakness and you can bring out the lion in me. the lion that

most people have never seen before and you make it happen so easily, so quick. but the lion roars because it loves. because it's afraid to lose the love that it's never going to find again, and because of that it protects and fights as soon as it needs to. no wasting time with thinking about it, just going after it. just going after the act of love.

10. You Are My Paradise

We look into each other's eyes.

Time stopped. Heartbeat fast.

We lean into each other.

Your nose touches mine.

Heave breaths. Close eyes.

We kiss.

Softly. Afraid that this won't last.

Your lips on mine.

God, is this paradise?

We separate.

My forehead touches yours.

You smile. I smile.

Your taste stays in my mouth.

The moment in my mind.

You hold my hand.

I rest my head on your shoulder.

Maybe, after all, this is paradise.

You and I.

11. Stop Running From Yourself

You can run away from yourself so often, and so much, just because the broken pieces of you cut your feet too deeply if you stay around for too long. But then what if someone were to come along and pick up those pieces for you? Then you wouldn't have to run away from yourself anymore. You could stop running. If someone sees you as something worth staying with maybe you'll stay with yourself, too.

12. Falling For You

You start relationship with someone.

She is getting more and more interesting every day.

You are falling.

Falling with little things.

Falling with laugh,

with talk,

with fingers,

with lips,

with smile,

with eyes,

with deep conversations at A.M

with music she shares with you

with art,

with museums you visit together,

with streets you walk with he,

with the way she smoke her cigarette,

with perfume,

with moments,

with her smell,

with tea you drank together,

with her favorite sweater of you,

with cafe you were together,

with movies you watched together,

with her family,

with her house,

with her favorite food.

You are falling in love.

And one day she has left.

You are falling a part.

You are all alone.

With everything she gave to you.

With memories.

And now - all that you have is your memories.

Only memories will be with you forever.

13. You Make My Memories

I look for you when I'm in car, singing to a song on the radio. I look for you when I'm drinking with friends, realizing that I'm so happy. I look for you when I'm laying in my bed and can't sleep for the life of me. I look for you when I'm watching a funny movie, laughing my head off. I look for you in all the photographs I have of myself. I look for you, in all the moments I wish you were there for. Because nothing would make me happier than singing, drinking, waking up and laughing with you. Living every piece of life with you. And the photographs; They were always better with you in them.

14. Maybe Love Is Just A Phase?

Maybe love stays. Maybe love can't. Maybe love shouldn't. Love arrives exactly when love is supposed to. And love leaves exactly when love must. When love arrives, say, 'Welcome. Make yourself comfortable.' If love leaves, ask her to leave the door open behind her. Turn off the music, listen to the quiet. Whisper, 'Thank you for stopping by.'

15. An Author

When life is unfair, strict or annoying, just grab a pen and a notebook and write.

Write about your feelings, write about your problems and dreams... Sometimes those checked or striped sheets of papers understand better than people.

16. He Don't Deserve You

You gave him so much of yourself. You gave him everything and still, he treated you as if none of it was good enough. The arguments, the tension, the late nights crying out of frustration. The overthinking about things that never deserved to be on your mind. It's fucked up, he fucked up, he hurt you and yet you apologized. He left you and you blamed your fucking self. There's nothing wrong with you! You can't keep things that don't deserve to stay. You can't find life in dead things. You can't find love, holding on to someone incapable of loving you. It's time to pick your fucking heart up off the ground and give the love you've wasted on him to yourself. You've been looking for a sign and this is it! Damn it, I just want you to be happy.

17. Accept Me The Way I Am

I remember when I was younger and I wanted to be beautiful; now I'm older and I want to be intelligent. I want to burn hearts with brilliance and engulf souls with compassion. I want to be loved for my thoughts and nothing else.

18. Were You Really The One?

I will never forgive you for the nights I stayed up crying and wondering why I wasn't good enough and I will never forgive you for the days where

my biggest accomplishment was getting out of bed. You broke my heart and
for that there is no space for any forgiveness. But I will sit here and thank
you, thank you for showing me I was worth more than you, thank you for
giving me the ultimate push to loving myself, thank you for showing me
you weren't the person I dreamt of you being. Here's to loving yourself after
a heartbreak. They leave because you need room to grow.

19. So I Am Not A Broken Heart

I am not the weight I lost or miles or ran and I am not the way I slept on
my doorstep under the bare sky in smell of tears and whiskey because my
apartment was empty and if I were to be this empty I wanted something
solid to sleep on. Like concrete.

I am not this year and I am not your fault. I am muscles building cells, a
little every day, because they broke that day, but bones are stronger once
they heal and I am smiling to the bus driver and replacing my groceries
once a week and I am not sitting for hours in the shower anymore. I am the
way a life unfolds and bloom and seasons come and go and I am the way
the spring always finds a way to turn even the coldest winter into a field of
green and flowers and new life.

I am not your fault.

20. Beauty In Armor

She's the kind of girl they write about in books. The kind with a fierce need for adventure, who isn't afraid to burst into the world and make all her dreams come true. She's the kind of girl with entire soliloquies dedicated to her smile, to the way those thin lips curl into a grin and knock the wind out of me every time. She's the kind of girl poems are penned for, with every detail on the page paying respect to her ways yet never quite capturing her true beauty and spirit.

21. Someone We Need

Maybe we're all just looking for someone who cares enough to try. Someone who has never had the best memory, but remembers the little things about you. Someone who has always been a little shy, but opens up to you. Someone who has never been good at keeping a conversation going, but can't shut up around you. Someone who hates driving on the highway, but spends hours on it to get to you. We're not hoping to change them. No, we're just hoping to matter enough to them.

Ten

1. Time Changes Everything

When we meet someone and fall in love, we have a sense that the whole universe is on our side. And yet if something goes wrong, there is nothing left! How is it possible for the beauty that was there only minutes before to vanish so quickly? Life moves very fast. It rushes from heaven to hell in a matter of seconds.

2. Let Me Be The One For You

Let me be the one. The one you recite jokes that you can't finish without laughing to. The one who makes you jam and butter toast because one is too bland and the other too sweet, so together they balance each other. The one who watches your favorite TV shows with you and keeps the first book that made you feel alive on their bookshelf. The one you turn to whenever you have a problem. The one you tell your crazy fantasies to, without thinking about how they make you look. Let me be the one. The one who can love you unashamedly. The one whom you trust with your pieces.

3. I Hope!!

I hope you remember my goofy smiles and stupid jokes. I hope you remember how messy my hair was in the morning. I hope you remember my favorite color and I hope some places still remind you of me. I hope that you smell my perfume somewhere in the street and you stop for a second wondering why was it so familiar to you. I hope sometimes when you kiss her those lips feel so strange, you think how I tasted. I hope her body doesn't feel like home to you, at least as much as mine felt. I hope that sometimes when you wake up in the middle of night and look at her peacefully sleeping beside you, you imagine every single feature of my face. I'm so sorry for being this unfair but I really hope that one day my absence disturbs you so much, you'll give up on her.

4. You Make Me Live Myself

You bring out the best in me. I don't mean better manners, or a sense of maturity, or whatever else this tired world expects of me. I mean you make me want to climb roofs, run wild, act inappropriately, take risks, and pursue my dreams with passion and integrity. Around you, I start living.

5. Someone

I hope you find someone who never makes you question your self-worth. I hope you find someone who chases your happiness as much as their own. I hope you find someone who supports you in the things you're passionate about. I hope you find someone whom you can laugh with, sit in silence with and share your deepest secrets with. I hope you find someone who is your lover, your partner and your friend. I hope you find someone who appreciates all the tiny details that make up who you are. I hope you find someone who respects your heart, your family and your values. I hope you find someone who reminds you that you deserve the love you give.

6. You Were Someone More Than I Deserved

And. I've known for a while now that someone like me isn't meant to be with someone like you. I am simply too much for you and in some cases, not enough. You wanted a light drizzle and I am a raging hurricane. Once again you have bit off a lot more than you can chew. You thought you could swallow me whole but you didn't realize I'd make you explode.

7. Apologization

Never apologize for how you feel. No one can control how they feel. The sun doesn't apologize for being the sun. The rain doesn't say sorry for falling. Feelings just are.

8. Who, How, What And Why?

Lately I've been thinking about who I want to love and how I want to love, and why I want to love the way I want to love, and what I need to learn to love that way, and who I need to become the kind of love I want to be.. and when I break it all down, when I whittle it into a single breath, it essentially comes out like this: Before I die, I want to be somebody's favorite hiding place, the place they can put everything they know they need to survive, every secret, every solitude, every nervous prayer, and be absolutely certain I will keep it safe. I will keep it safe.

9. Reasons Why you should LOVE YOURSELF

1) Everyone might leave at one point of time when their interest disappears or they find a better person.

2) You will learn to enjoy your own company even if there comes tough times or you're left alone.

3) Reading books, watching web or tv series or even cooking yourself a good food aren't really bad ideas at all.

4) You'll not feel bad if you're not invited for a party or your so-called friends made a plan without you.

5) You'll learn how to fight things without the support of anyone so whenever you get a life partner or a Best friend they'll already have someone to inspire them.

6) If you fall down due to circumstances youll know how to inspire yourself and get up like a flying star.

7) You will learn to handle heart breaks and you'll never give up your self respect for some egoistic person.

8) People will be shocked to see that in this world where almost everyone is damaged or crying due to betrayals you're the one who's aspiring everyone to become self independent like you.

9) Lastly,if you cannot love yourself then how can you expect somebody else to love you.

10. Can I Forgive!?

Should I forgive you? Everytime I felt low, You were not here with me. Should i forgive you for that? For being so carefree. I used to call you all day, My call was always declined. Should I forgive you for that? For being busy on some other line. Even after all the fights, I always gave it a try. Should I forgive you for that? For making my heart cry. I never asked for anything, Just you to love me till your last breath. Should I forgive you for that? For killing me before my death. You left without even thinking, Drifted apart with so much ease. Should I forgive you for that? For breaking me in different different piece. Those nights still haunt me, I used to scream with tears.

Should I forgive you for that?

For giving me those lifelong fears.

I was waiting for you at the shore,

And you disappeared like the waves of the sea.

11. Take Your Own Time

Don't overthink

Don't worry

Just take your time

No need to hurry

It's just a phase

It's just the life

You'll be fine

You'll be alright

No need to give up

Better you retry

You'll get the success

You'll touch the sky

Listen to your heart

Listen to your mind

No need to get frustrated

Just be humble and kind

I know you're capable

I know you're smart

Go, give your efforts

And just top the chart

I know you get scared

I know you lose hope

But do something crazy

And just be a dope.

I'm there with you

No matter how the situations are

I'll never leave your hand

I'll never be ashamed of your scars

No need of leaving

When the love is true

Darkness is just temporary

The sky will again be blue

So there's no need to give up

Better you retry

You'll get the success

You'll touch the sky.

12. When I'm Gone

When I'm gone;

They'll burn my body

Maybe they'll forget my soul

But the words I am writing here

I would leave them

For the world to read

To feel my pain

To live my happiness

To see my love

To break the chain

They'll read my verse

But I won't be there

Maybe they'll feel guilty

But I won't care

They'll set fire to my body

And the river will taste my bone

Maybe they'll miss me

Maybe they'll cry for me

But I won't care

Because I'll be gone.

13. Let Me Move On

Leave the light on,

So I can assemble me

Whom she killed

Ever day and night

Now I want to stand

And win that fight.

Leave the light on,

So I can see the demons

Hidden within my heart

I want to talk to them tonight

And convince them to leave my world.

Leave the light on,

So I can analyse the anxiety

And depression I'm facing since a year

I'll throw them away

And will cheers with the beer.

Leave the light on,

As I've seen the things

I never wanted to see

Now this is the time

To change myself

And be what I always wanted to be.

14. Everyone's Darkside

Yes, we all hide our pain, we all have a dark side, about which we never speak out loud, yes,we do hide our pain. Life teaches us many things and so does time as well. Life teaches us how to face all the odds by smiling, no matter how complicated the situation gets ever. Everyone out there have their own dark, untold story and each one has a different way to deal with it. Why do you think I became a writer? Well, it's because I too had a time when times weren't good and I was surrounded by negetive vibes. An artist tells about their own self to the world by their ar and few people hit the gym to remove their anger. It's often said "never judge a book by it's cover", and the same goes for a person who is smiling from outside yet dying inside. So it's better not to judge anyone without knowing their story as at the end of the day, everyone fights through their own, untold battles..

15. It's Okay To Be Not Okay

Does a hey-I'm-alright note

succeed in making you okay

even when you're fighting

endless battles and aren't okay at all?

Hiding tears behind your nerdy specs

you dig your face into books,

fearing your brother's concern queries..

You're not okay whenever

you find anything relatabe & your heart kicks your stomach, yet

you hide your tears with stupid excuses like

"Mom-I-was-cutting-onions" or

"Dad-something-went-into-my-eye". You're not okay and

accepting that is absolutely okay.

The sun can't blush in hues of ochre and red daily,

the moon can't appear full even on days when it's rainy,

you can't find apples and strawberries in every season,

you can't let your misery overpower you often..

You're not okay when your classmate calls you for notes and your eyes glue

to your scarred wrists or to the crippled breakup letter.

You can't abandon your emotions always,

because you-too-are-a-freaking-human.

You ought to feel everything you want to,

you are supposed to feel vulnerable at times,

you're allowed to spend nights by just crying and staring at the ceiling by

doing nothing and that's OKAY. .

It's okay to feel vulnerable,

clueless and helpless at times,

Not all days are same,

not all fingers on a hand are same,

not all battles we go through are easy.

But, everything which doesn't make us okay is moulding the

clay of our fragility into perfection which is taking a lot of time and giving

endless pain,

yet THAT'S COMPLETELY OKAY. .

16. My Feelings In A Poem

I date my words

and dance with my poems,

Holding hands,

Matching vibes

and by doing steps

On the clean floor.

No, no, that's not enough

I've just started,

and I want to touch it

to the core.

I want to move it,

I want to arrange it,

I want it to get rhymed,

explaining the essence

And the flowing emotions

In every sentence,

and every stanza.

I want it to get on my nerves

And make me high

Just like how drugs

do it with its intakers.

I want to live it,

I want to feel it

And want to present it

As my lover,

In front of the world.

I don't want it

For a few days or months,

But I want to be in love

With my poetries forever.

Because this is the only love

and lover, I care about.

17. Perks Of Being A One Sided Lover

1. There's no game of expectations, you'll not get hurt randomly.

2. You can talk to them without the fear of being judged bypeople around you.

3. You can proudly call yourself single, inspite of being in love.

4. You can always make new crushes and no one will stop you.

5. Looking into their eyes secretly and blushing when theysmile, will always tickle you.

6. You'll always enjoy it when your friends will tease you infront of them and you try to stop them although unwantedly.

7. There's no chance of heartbreak, you can always look attheir pictures and be happy.

8. You can take out time for other hobbies of your intereststoo, you needn't worry about giving time to them.

9. You'll always feel good about your love, that it's so pure and selfless.

18. WHY?

It's been so long since we broke up.

So long, that I finally thought I'm not holding onto you anymore and that
I've moved on.

But it's strange how I still get all those flashbacks.

Your memories flood in my mind and those tears still kickback.

Why do I still smile,

when I think about our good days?

Why does my heart beat faster, even when we have parted

ways since a while?

Why does your name, still turn my head?

Why is there still a hope, after everything's done and is said?

I'm so clinged to these memories,

I can't break them loose,

it's like a part of you in me,

like permanent tattoos.

What am I still holding on?

Why am I still stuck?

What do I call this feeling?

A feeling that's been plucked.

Am I really twisted?

These feelings don't seem new

for darkness doesn't haunt me,

but your memories do.

19. *This Is My Love story*

This is not a poem,

rather an unboxing

of all the unsaid complaints about you

which I've been doing to myself,

with a hope of feeling less guilty

about the ifs and buts in place of maybes,

about wanting to say that I'm dying from within but not before you care
enough to enquire

and longing for you to send me a hey-are-you-alright text.

This is not a poem

about how we parted ways

or about how you'd kept me caged,

it's more of an apology to my past self

for allowing myself to feel vulnerable,

for not owing myself enough respect

to cut you off from my life and

let go off the love which I kept giving,

even if with a heavy heart and bleeding skin.

Every night,

I survive on the last sip of caffeine

to trigger enough courage within me,

so that I can confront you of your sins,

of the fake yet sweet-and-sour allegations

and of the you-fucked-up-my-life tag.

Days have been darker

and nights have been lonelier,

no amount of cigars, shots or caffeine could lessen the pain of your
departure.

Yet, with a heavy heart and a numb soul,

I'm ready again to take the road not taken,

amidst the bridges of betrayals and buds of hope,

but this time; after unboxing the letters of

your sins, because this is not a poem,

it's my freaking bleeding heart

which cries to let out the unspoken truth.

20. The End

There are some people in my life

who handled me when I was in the

most critical condition of my life

neglecting what was going in their own life.

I never made them realise that

how much they matter in my life.

This is one of the biggest guilts

which has been heaped on my

heart. But now I want to tell them

that they were and are the most

honest and caring persons in my

life. Thank you for staying and not

allowing me give up on this life.

Author's Note

As I have done a lot mistakes in relationship, after my first heartbreak I have taken her for granted that she's always mine or whatever happens she needs to stay. Just don't take your love for granted it hurts your love, he/she just expect your love, caring and importancy. I always regret for not giving this things to my love as I am very short tempered and having anger issues. I realised this mistakes after she left me unharmed. She was just expecting and hoping for my love everyday and I didn't gave anything. Don't ignore your love, it hurts, don't do this mistakes' in your relationship. Never beat your love. I will always be guilty forever for what I've done. If possible communicate and get this things out of your life after he/she gets his true realisation and forgive him/her for their mistake.

Thank You Note

You turned pages, read each word and ultimately you've reached here.
I hope the journey till here was as I expected, full of adrenaline and
oxytocin.
I hope you could feel the Love and Heartbreak.
Now that you have reached the end, I want a little favour from you. You
read my book and I hope you liked it. It would mean the world to me if you
took out a minute and gave your feedback on this book. You can do so by
sharing it on social media platforms like FACEBOOK and INSTAGRAM.
You may tag "@nynlofi" and "@lofinyn" on INSTAGRAM and tell me
how you liked the book. This small favour will help me to improve in the
future and I will be able to deliver something much better than this
anthology book. Your support will help me reach a larger crowd.
Thanks for being with me in this journey, it's because of you that I never
stop.